BABE's
COUNTRY COOKBOOK

BABE's
COUNTRY COOKBOOK
80 COMPLETELY MEAT-FREE RECIPES!

Text and recipes by **DEWEY GRAM**

Photographs by **MARTIN JACOBS**

GT
PUBLISHING
NEW YORK

EDITOR
David Ricketts

DESIGNER
Barbara Marks

RECIPE TESTERS
Elaine Khosrova, Michael Krondl,
Paul Piccuito, Sarah Reynolds

COPY EDITOR AND PROOFREADER
Stephen Robert Frankel

RECIPE COPY EDITOR
Stephanie Grozdea

INDEXER
Catherine Dorsey

FOOD SAFETY SPECIALIST
Elizabeth L. Andress, Ph.D.

PHOTOGRAPHER
Martin Jacobs

FOOD STYLIST
Polly Talbott

ASSISTANT FOOD STYLIST
Carrie Orthner

PROP STYLIST
Linda Johnson

ANIMALS APPEARING IN PHOTOGRAPHS
Farm animals, courtesy Cornell
Cooperative Extension, Yaphank, NY.
Puppies, courtesy Terry Sadler's Sterling
Borders. Kittens, courtesy "Being Kind"
Animal Rescue.

Photographs copyright © 1998 Martin Jacobs
Text and recipes by Dewey Gram

Published in 1998 by GT Publishing Corporation
16 E. 40th Street, New York, NY 10016

Library of Congress Cataloging-in-Publication Data

Gram, Dewey.
    Babe's country cookbook : 80 completely meat-free
recipes / text and recipes by Dewey Gram : photographs by
Martin Jacobs.
        p.   cm.
    Includes index.
    ISBN: 1-57719-354-7 (hardcover)
      1. Vegetarian cookery.   I. Title.
TX837.G6734   1998
641.5'636—dc21   98-24933
                                                                        CIP

ISBN: 1-57719-354-7

Printed in Singapore

1 3 5 7 9 10 8 6 4 2
First Printing

Contents

Babe-Approved Suppers, Every Which Way 103

"EVERY MEAL IS A FEAST—MY MUM'S OWN WORDS, THEY ARE. SHE WAS A TRIFLE ROLY-POLY HERSELF, GOODNESS YES."

Esme Pickles with Relish 127

"DON'T BE THINKING YOU CAN JUST GO OUT AND BUY THESE OFF A SHELF! OH, NO!"

Something Sweet from Paradise 139

"BAKING IS THE SOUL OF COUNTRY LIFE."

Introduction

Kitchens, as everyone knows, have hearts. And within these pages is a Babe's-eye view of the heart of the Hoggett kitchen, the lively corner of the Hoggett Family Farm that keeps the whole place humming.

There are the recipes, of course: the best of Esme Hoggett's wonderful country food. But here also is the savor of these good people in their farm home, with their simple truths out of the mouths of Babe and his human and animal friends.

Just as Babe is a prize-winning sheep-pig, so Mrs. Hoggett is a Grand National Blue Ribbon Cook and Baker. (And, well, a champion eater, too.) Babe gives us eighty recipes from Esme Hoggett's kitchen, mostly her own prize dishes, and a few special ones from relatives and friends and from fans in faraway places.

Real Country Cooking

"Most everybody is a city dweller nowadays, oh my, yes," Esme says, "but your country roots are not so distant. Your Mother's classic home cooking, her Mother's before her—your all-time favorite dishes? Where do you think those recipes originally came from? Why, from a farm cook's kitchen, that's where!"

Country cookery is what Babe and Esme share with you in this book, but with shades of difference.

Bushels of up-to-date ingredients and ideas, for one thing.

Esme isn't locked in the past. To the contrary, she has a wickedly roving eye and an adventurous palate. It was impossible to keep her wholly down on the farm once she'd discovered Parmigiano Reggiano, or basmati rice, or *Sambal Olek* chili-garlic paste.

Babe and Esme have also exercised a little trimming. They've selected recipes that are, overall, a *little* less filling than typical country food. Authentic farm fare, yes—bursting with vitamin-rich fresh vegetables, home-picked fruits, just-snipped herbs, dairy-fresh cheeses. But a scooch less butter here, easy on the salt there; *ix-nay* on heavy, creamy casseroles, *oui* to lighter, savory sauces.

Still, some decadent recipes have slipped in—let's admit that right up front: splurge foods, once-a-month indulgences for the sane contemporary eater.

A Ticklish Issue

There is another somewhat . . . *delicate* issue Babe would like aired here.

You will remember that when Babe first came to Hoggett Farm, Mrs. Hoggett eyed his plump haunches and began feeding him lavishly. "My, my! All these lovely vittles! What a lucky little pork chop you are! Yum, yum! *De*-licious!"

Babe soon learned the dreadful truth behind this posh treatment. It lay in the Established Order of Things. Dogs were for herding sheep, sheep were for wool, cows for milking, chickens for egg-laying, and ducks and pigs . . . for Christmas dinner! "What could we do with a pig, eh Duchess?" he heard Mrs. Hoggett say, licking her lips. "Just think—two nice hams, two sides of bacon, pork chops, kidneys, liver, chitlins, pickle his feet, save his blood for black pudding . . ."

Babe, as all the world knows, found the idea of Main Dish as Destiny to be *unpalatable!* And he set about, with pluck and an open heart, to change the Established Order of Things. Far from ending up as Roast Suckling Treat *du Jour*, Babe won the National Grand Challenge Sheep Dog Trials and carved out a glorious new place for himself on the Farm. And not as bacon-in-waiting. By no means. And by his gifts, he brought something of still greater significance to the Farm: Compassion for *all* living things. Compassion for animals! He gave a fresh lease on life to all his barnyard friends.

Esme Hoggett, long a casual carnivore, took an abrupt turn toward the vegetarian. No more Ferdinand *à l'Orange* on *her* Christmas menu! "Eating Babe's friends would be—oh-my-gosh, oh-deary-me—barbaric!"

So, yes, Babe's book is a *meat-free* farm cookbook—perhaps as rare a bird as the Grand National Sheep-Pig himself. You could stamp it on every page: 100% Animal-Friendly!

Hearty Farm Breakfasts

"Piggy-piggy-piggy-piggy! Breakfast!"

Esme's breakfast board: overstuffed omelets, buttery scones, sizzling hash browns, wedges of yesterday's fruit cobbler—anything that will stick to the ribs and get the day off with a bang.

"If you think breakfast isn't a big meal on the farm, well you've got another think coming," Esme Hoggett pronounces. "Coffee and a bagel? You must be daft! Farm folk *eat* in the morning." Indeed, farm people have to stoke the fires high between the first round of chores in the frigid pre-dawn and the mountain of work to come.

Some of the most delicious food made in Esme Hoggett's kitchen comes out at first light: Best-of-Show Popovers, Scottish Oat Scones, Poppy Seed Bread with Lemon-Butter Glaze, Honey Oatmeal Muffins, spicy Hot Cross Buns with Maple Icing, scrumptious Old-Fashioned Cornmeal Mush, and for special occasions, Bishop's Bread.

And then there's the open secret about farm breakfasts: The folks don't care if what they eat is breakfast food only by name, and is really best suited for the evening meal. Pies, tarts, and other sweet baked goods are top sellers at farm town cafes at 8 A.M., right up there with fried potatoes and egg platters.

Babe, from his spot by the doggy door, watches an equally wide variety of foods appear on Esme's breakfast board, including some desserts left over from the evening before, such as fruit tortes, wedges of rhubarb-custard pie, and even a scoop of cobbler (see the desserts chapter, "Something Sweet from Paradise," page 139). Some Hoggett Farm All-Time Greatest Hits breakfasts are here, the wee pig will tell you—he never misses an Esme breakfast.

Babe's Porcini Omelet with Feta Cheese and Fresh Sage

It's "Babe's" because porcini in Italian, *naturalmente*, is "little pig." And yes, in homage to him, Mrs. H. always makes two omelets—one for the table, one for Babe's bowl. "He smiles when he's eating it," she says. "Of course he knows! He heard me say the porcini is *the* great mushroom for Italians, and now he won't touch another kind. Oh, maybe a nice morel now and then—if it's fresh." Compounding the earthy allure of the porcini here is the pungent flavor and bouquet of the freshly chopped sage and the tang of the scallions, garlic, and feta cheese. This is an omelet for company—or Babe.

1 large porcini or other wild mushroom, or even button mushrooms

1/4 cup olive oil

2 scallions, including an inch of the green part, thinly sliced

1 clove garlic, finely chopped

1 tablespoon chopped fresh sage leaves, or 1 teaspoon dried

6 large eggs

1/4 cup water

1/2 teaspoon salt, or to taste

1/4 teaspoon freshly ground black pepper, or to taste

2 tablespoons unsalted butter

Rinse and cut the porcini into 1/2-inch dice. In a roomy skillet, heat the olive oil over medium heat. Add the mushrooms, and cook over medium heat for 2 to 3 minutes, or until slightly softened.

Add the scallions, garlic, and sage and continue cooking until the mushroom pieces are light golden brown, 2 to 3 minutes. Spoon the mushroom mixture into a strainer to drain off the extra liquid.

In a large bowl, whisk together the eggs with the water, salt, and pepper until well blended.

In a medium-size nonstick omelet pan, heat 1 tablespoon of the butter, swirling the butter around the bottom of the pan. Once the hot butter's foaming begins to slow down, you're ready to go—don't let the butter brown.

(continued)

*Babe's Porcini Omelet with Feta Cheese and Fresh Sage
and Honey Oatmeal Muffins*

6 *tablespoons crumbled feta cheese*

Pour half the egg-water mixture into the hot pan. As the edges begin to set, lift them with a spatula and tilt the pan so that all the liquidy egg runs under the bottom and cooks. When the eggs are just set, spoon half the porcini-scallion-garlic mixture into the center, and then add half the crumbled feta.

Gently fold half the omelet over the filling. Tip the pan and slide or turn the omelet onto a warmed plate. Serve immediately.

Repeat with the remaining ingredients to make the second omelet.

Serve with a baguette and sweet butter, or a breakfast pastry such as Esme's Apricot Coffee Cake with Streusel Filling (page 24), Honey Oatmeal Muffins (below), or Feather Rolls (page 32) with a jar of fruit preserves.

MAKES 2 PORTIONS (2 OMELETS)

Honey Oatmeal Muffins

His minimum is four: two for breakfast, one for each side pocket to see him through the long morning. That's Arthur Hoggett's bottom line when it comes to his wife's celestial, Sunday-only honey oatmeal muffins. Mrs. H. came by the recipe at the University of the Domestic Arts: Her mother-in-law, on the day of her wedding, slapped a slip of paper in Esme's hand as she was departing the premises and pronounced cryptically, "You'll need these." Arthur Hoggett, it appears, is a hard sleeper. The sweet, orchardy smell of hot honey oatmeal muffins wafting up the stairs is, to this day, the *only* way to get him to church on wintry Sunday mornings.

1 1/2 cups old-fashioned rolled oats or quick-cooking oats
1 cup all-purpose flour
1/2 cup raisins
1/2 cup chopped nuts, such as walnuts or pecans
1/3 cup firmly packed brown sugar
1 tablespoon baking powder
3/4 teaspoon salt
2/3 cup milk
1/3 cup vegetable oil
1 large egg, beaten
1/4 cup honey

Preheat your oven to 400°. Grease or line with paper cups 12 standard-size muffin-pan cups.

In an ample bowl, stir together the oats, flour, raisins, nuts, sugar, baking powder, and salt.

In another bowl, stir together the milk, oil, beaten egg, and honey. Stir the milk mixture into the oat mixture just until the dry ingredients are moistened. Mustn't overmix muffin batter, or you'll get those unsightly tunnels when they're baked. Fill the muffin cups about two-thirds full.

Bake in the 400° oven for 15 to 18 minutes, or until the muffins turn golden brown and a wooden pick inserted in the centers comes out clean. Turn the muffins out onto a wire rack to cool.

Serve hot with butter, maple syrup, or honey, or just plain with cups of warming cappuccino. Makes a great accompaniment to Babe's Porcini Omelet with Feta Cheese and Fresh Sage (page 10).

MAKES 12 MUFFINS (REGULAR SIZE, WHICH ARE BETTER FOR STUFFING IN POCKETS)

Old-Fashioned Cornmeal Mush

"Hooo-eeee! Children!" It's the call on chill winter mornings, or after hours of sledding when cold little cheeks need warming, that brings Mrs. Hoggett's grandchildren into the kitchen for a steaming bowl of golden cornmeal mush, sprinkled with brown sugar or splashed with maple syrup. An indispensable country staple, cornmeal was cooked up by the American Indians, and the settlers carried it with them as they made their way west—a handy substitute for hard-to-get white flour. And it's no less appreciated by Mrs. Hoggett—she makes it up as a different kind of treat when she serves slices of it, fried, topped with butter, honey, or sorghum. Farmer Hoggett himself likes it this way for dinner, sliced and fried, but topped with grated cheese or potato gravy (see Hosenhorne, page 111). "Why, it's fearfully simple to make," Mrs. Hoggett says. Now and then she lets Mr. Hoggett into the kitchen *completely unattended* to whip some up.

3 *cups water*
1 *cup yellow cornmeal*
1 *teaspoon salt*
1 *cup cold water*
Vegetable oil or butter, if you're frying slices of mush
Brown sugar, honey, sorghum, or maple syrup, for a sweet topping (optional)

In a saucepan, heat the 3 cups of water to boiling. In a small bowl, stir together the cornmeal, salt, and cold water. Pour the cornmeal mixture gradually into the boiling water, stirring constantly—this method helps prevent lumping during cooking. Bring back to a boil, then cook, stirring occasionally, over low heat for 5 to 8 minutes, or until oatmeal consistency.

Serve in bowls with a little milk and brown sugar or maple syrup.

To serve in slices for dinner, pour the mush while still hot into a lightly greased glass or ceramic loaf pan (an aluminum or other reactive pan will discolor the yellow cornmeal) and chill in the refrigerator for 2 or 3 hours or overnight. The mush will become solid but spongy.

Turn the solid mush out onto a work surface and cut crosswise into 1/2-inch-thick slices. Fry in vegetable oil or butter in a roomy skillet for 4 or 5 minutes per side, or until lightly browned. Top with brown sugar, honey, sorghum, or maple syrup, and serve hot.

MAKES 6 BOWLSFUL, OR A LOAF, CUT INTO 8 TO 10 SLICES

Hash Browns with Wild Mushrooms and Cream

The mistress of Hoggett Farm prepares this dish after the Man of the House has come back from foraging in the dead leaves of the oak and spruce forest beyond the sheep pastures. When he brings back a sack of chanterelles, it is with the anticipation of waking to the earthy, nutty smell of roasting mushrooms and garlic the next morning. Making Yankee classic hash brown potatoes is an art, and the starting point is good, raw potatoes. Here the browned potatoes and onions roast in the mushroom-garlic sauce long enough to absorb the flavors but not lose their crispy, crunchy texture. Chanterelles can be bought almost everywhere now.

4 large red new potatoes (about 2 pounds)
3 tablespoons vegetable oil
1/2 cup chopped onion

MAKING THE HASH BROWNS: Peel and cut up the potatoes into 1/2-inch dice. In a large skillet, or 2 medium-size, heat the oil to sizzling. Stir in the onion. Add the potatoes and stir to coat them with the oil, and spread in an even layer over the bottom. Reduce the heat to low. Cook slowly, giving the pan an occasional jog to prevent sticking,

(continued)

2 tablespoons unsalted butter

1 cup fresh chanterelles or other mushrooms, such as shiitake or baby portobello, wiped clean and cut into large pieces

2 cloves garlic, finely chopped

1/2 cup heavy cream

1/4 cup sour cream

3/4 teaspoon salt

1/2 teaspoon freshly ground black pepper

1 cup shredded Gruyère cheese

until the bottom of the potato "pancake" is browned, about 30 minutes. The timing will all depend on the size of your skillet and the heat. When brown, turn the "pancake" over and cook a bit longer, until browned and crusty.

Preheat your oven to 350°.

In a large ovenproof saucepan or Dutch oven, melt the butter. Add the mushrooms and garlic, and sauté over medium heat for 2 minutes. Add the cream, and boil until reduced by half, about 3 minutes. Stir in the sour cream, and then carefully stir in the hash browns and the salt and pepper.

Bake the hash browns in the 350° oven for 15 minutes. Sprinkle the cheese over the top, and bake for 5 minutes more. Remove from the oven, and serve piping hot.

A hearty accompaniment to morning eggs, or with soup or salad later in the day.

SERVES 8 HUNGRY FARMHANDS

Blue Ribbon Banana-Nut-Lemon Bread

This makes a very moist, fruity, dark banana bread. "Too-o-o delicious," Mrs. H. says. The Boss and Babe both prefer their banana bread toasted and, if Mrs. lets them get away with it, dotted with melting sweet butter. This bread won the Best of Class Blue Ribbon at five different area competitions before Esme retired it. "It just seemed fair—not to mention good sense," she says. "Remember the old adage: 'Pull all your sweet potatoes today, sauerkraut tomorrow!'"

2   large eggs

1/2   cup vegetable oil

3   small or 2 medium very ripe bananas, peeled and cut up

1/2   teaspoon grated lemon zest

1   teaspoon fresh lemon juice

2   cups all-purpose flour

1   cup granulated white sugar

1   teaspoon baking soda

1/2   teaspoon salt

3/4   cup chopped nutmeats, such as walnuts, almonds, or pecans, or whatever you like

Preheat your oven to 350°.

Place the eggs, vegetable oil, bananas, and lemon zest and juice in a blender, and whirl until smooth.

In a large bowl, stir together the flour, sugar, baking soda, and salt. Pour the banana mixture along with the nuts into the flour mixture, and stir just until combined, being careful not to overmix. Pour batter into a 9 × 5 × 3-inch loaf pan.

Bake in the 350° oven for about 1 hour, or until the top is golden brown and a wooden pick inserted in the center comes out clean.

Transfer the pan to a wire rack and let sit for 10 minutes. Then turn the bread out onto the rack to cool. Slice with a serrated knife.

Serve while still warm or at room temperature with fresh sweet butter, or just plain. Or, when no one's looking, try it with a smear of peanut butter.

MAKES 1 LOAF, 8 TO 10 SLICES

Poppy Seed Bread with Lemon-Butter Glaze,
Hot Cross Buns with Maple Icing,
and Scottish Oat Scones

Scottish Oat Scones

Both Mr. and Mrs. Hoggett prefer scones in the morning to plain biscuits. Perhaps it's because of the rich, buttery taste—the egg and milk, the bit of sugar. Scones (pronounced *skahns*) came originally from Scotland by way of early settlers in Nova Scotia. Since they are "quick breads," they need no kneading and rising time (using the faster baking powder instead of yeast), and they can be baked just as easily on a greased griddle or in a hot oven. Mrs. H. has seen many kinds of scones entered in area competitions—orange, prune, date, basil, potato, whole wheat, onion—but she turns up her nose at them. "I prefer real Scottish scones," she says, "made with oats, wedge-shaped, and served with my preserves or a lick of sweet butter."

1 1/2 cups all-purpose flour
1/4 cup granulated white sugar
1 tablespoon baking powder
1 teaspoon cream of tartar
1/2 teaspoon salt
1/2 cup (1 stick) unsalted butter, cut into small pieces
1 1/4 cups old-fashioned rolled oats
1 cup dried currants, raisins, or dried cranberries
1 large egg
1/3 cup milk

Preheat your oven to 375°. Grease a baking sheet.

In an ample bowl, mix the flour, sugar, baking powder, cream of tartar, and salt. With a pastry blender or 2 knives held like a scissors, cut in the butter until the mixture looks like bread crumbs. Stir in oats and dried fruit. Make a well in center.

In another bowl, mix egg and milk, and pour into well in dry ingredients. With a fork, stir wet ingredients into dry, until everything is evenly moistened and comes together in a ball. (Be careful—overhandling will make scones tough.) The dough should be soft and crumbly.

Pat the dough out on a lightly floured board to form an 8-inch circle. Transfer to the greased baking sheet. With a knife dipped into flour, cut into 12 equal wedges.

(continued)

TOPPING
1 *tablespoon milk*
2 *tablespoons granulated white sugar*

FOR THE TOPPING: Brush wedges with the milk, and then sprinkle with the sugar.

Bake in the 375° oven 22 to 25 minutes, until golden brown.

Serve warm from the oven. Split in half, and serve with marmalade, honey, or apple butter—and English tea. For a special treat, try them with clotted cream. Besides serving scones with morning or afternoon coffee or tea, Esme uses them in her strawberry shortcake. Well, why not?

MAKES 12 SCONES

Poppy Seed Bread with Lemon-Butter Glaze

It's a sea of pink and white flowers in June—the Hoggett Farm poppy field. During the first warm days of March, Esme can be seen out there bustling, planting, and chattering to the sheep peering over the fence: "Oh, I was worried we'd have a late spring, weren't you? My, my. Ruin the schedule! Late tomatoes, peppers, late poppies! It's turned quite splendid, don't you think? But if you muttonheads put so much as a nose over that fence, it's the stew pot!" In early summer, Babe and the animals watch the Mrs. harvest her own poppy flowers and perform a curious ritual. She snaps off the heads, knifes a slit in them, and shakes tiny purple-blue kernels out of the pods. She painstakingly picks out the imperfect ones, washes the rest, and then hangs them up in a cloth bag in the summer sun to dry—"in the tallest tree in the yard, out of reach of my greedy chickens and ducks." Esme is a true poppy seed devotee.

BREAD

3 large eggs, lightly beaten
3/4 cup vegetable oil
1 1/2 teaspoons vanilla extract
1 teaspoon almond extract
2 1/4 cups granulated white
    sugar
3 cups all-purpose flour
2 teaspoons baking powder
1 1/2 teaspoons salt
2 tablespoons poppy seeds
    (if you don't dry your own,
    store-bought are fine)
1 1/2 cups milk

GLAZE

3/4 cup confectioners' sugar
1/4 cup orange juice
1 tablespoon unsalted butter
1/2 teaspoon grated lemon zest
1 teaspoon fresh lemon juice
1/2 teaspoon vanilla extract

MAKING THE BREAD: Preheat your oven to 350°. Grease and flour two 8 × 4-inch loaf pans.

In an ample bowl, stir together the eggs, oil, vanilla and almond extracts, and sugar.

In another bowl, mix together the flour, baking powder, salt, and poppy seeds. Add the egg mixture and the milk to the flour mixture, stirring until well blended. Then pour the batter into the prepared pans, dividing evenly.

Bake the breads in the 350° oven for about 65 to 75 minutes. The bread is done when it turns golden brown, pulls away slightly from the sides of the pan, and a wooden pick inserted in the center comes out clean. Transfer the pans to a wire rack and let them sit for 10 minutes. Then turn the breads out onto the rack and let them cool completely.

MAKING THE GLAZE: Combine all the ingredients for the glaze in a saucepan and place the pan over medium-high heat, bringing the mixture to a boil. Then boil for 1 minute. Slide a piece of waxed paper under the wire rack, under the breads, to catch any drips. Brush the glaze over the top and sides of the loaves, letting it soak in. Let the breads stand until the glaze sets.

Serve at breakfast with a crock of sweet butter and mugs of freshly brewed coffee, or at afternoon tea with a jar of orange or lemon marmalade.

MAKES 2 LOAVES, ABOUT 10 SLICES PER LOAF

Hot Cross Buns with Maple Icing

It is a mystery why some food items drop out of favor. These old-fashioned Easter-time delicacies have not been a standard cookbook item for more than half a century. Served once a year in England on Good Friday, hot cross buns were an indispensable part of the Easter ritual. If the reaction of Mrs. Hoggett's grandchildren is any indication, the sweet rolls are due for a rebirth. "Do they favor them? Why, a dozen at a sitting! You'd think the poor tots were starving." Once you've tasted authentic hot cross buns, you'll understand. The subtle, spicy aroma will forever tickle your memory: cinnamon, cloves, nutmeg, allspice. The Hoggett Farm recipe offers a tiny variation on the classic: a light maple icing instead of plain white sugar frosting.

BUNS

- 1 envelope active dry yeast
- 1/4 cup warm water (105° to 115°)
- 1 cup warm milk (105° to 115°)
- 1/4 cup granulated white sugar
- 3 tablespoons light-brown sugar
- 1 teaspoon salt
- 2 large eggs, lightly beaten
- 1/2 teaspoon vanilla extract
- 1/2 cup (1 stick) unsalted butter, melted
- 3 1/2 to 4 1/2 cups all-purpose flour

MAKING THE BUNS: In an ample bowl, sprinkle the yeast over the warm water, and let stand until the mixture is foamy, about 5 minutes (if the yeast doesn't foam, start over; see page 32). Stir to dissolve the yeast. Then stir in the milk, white sugar, brown sugar, salt, eggs, vanilla, and 6 tablespoons of the melted butter.

Add 3 1/2 cups flour, the cinnamon, nutmeg, cloves, allspice, and, if using, the currants. Beat well with a wooden spoon. Gradually stir in enough of the remaining flour to make a very soft dough.

Remove the dough from the bowl to a floured work surface. Knead the dough with your hands for several minutes until it's smooth and resilient, adding just enough flour as needed to keep it from sticking to your hands or the work surface. Place dough in a buttered bowl, cover with clean towel, and let sit in a warm place until doubled in size, about 2 hours.

3/4 teaspoon ground
   cinnamon
1/2 teaspoon freshly grated
   nutmeg
1/4 teaspoon ground cloves
1/4 teaspoon ground allspice
1/2 cup dried currants
   (optional)

ICING
1 cup confectioners' sugar
1 tablespoon milk
1/4 teaspoon maple extract

Punch the dough down and knead it briefly on a floured surface. Shape the dough into a 9 × 9-inch square, about 1 inch thick, and using a sharp knife, cut the dough into about 25 to 30 equal squares.

Place the squares 1 1/2 inches apart on greased baking sheets, half the squares to each sheet. Cover, and let rise again until doubled in size, 1 to 1 1/2 hours.

Preheat your oven to 350°. With a very sharp knife or single-edge razor blade, cut a cross in the top of each bun. Brush the top of each with the remaining 2 tablespoons of melted butter. Bake the buns in the 350° oven for 16 to 18 minutes, until the buns turn golden on top. About halfway through the baking, reverse the baking sheets in the oven, from front to back, and from one oven rack to another. When done, transfer the buns to a wire rack to cool.

MAKING THE ICING: In a small mixing bowl, whisk together the confectioners' sugar, milk, and maple extract. Add a little more milk if needed to make a good drizzling consistency. Drizzle the icing onto the buns, following the design of the cross. To make it easy, spoon the icing into a small plastic bag, snip off one tiny corner, and then pipe the icing onto the buns.

Set these out on a plate while they're still warm, and stand back. Esme's grandchildren love them with hot chocolate.

MAKES 25 TO 30 BUNS, ENOUGH FOR THE GRANDCHILDREN

Apricot Coffee Cake with Streusel Filling

"The" classic coffee cake brought to Hoggett perfection. Esme sometimes adds a layer of fresh apricots, or other fruits she can pick in season—but for year-round pleasure, you can use canned or preserved fruit. "Streusel" is the German word for the mixture of flour, sugar, butter, cinnamon, and chopped nuts that fills the crevices and hollows in the top of the coffee cake and makes it so mouth-watering. In Mrs. H.'s recipe, the streusel is layered in the middle of the cake as well. And here's one Hoggett kitchen secret for great coffee cake: "Separate bowls," Esme says. "One for dry ingredients, one for wet." Combine them only seconds before you commit to a preheated oven, so that the batter will do all of its rising while baking, not while languishing on the work table. A lighter, moister cake is the reward.

STREUSEL FILLING

- 1/2 cup firmly packed brown sugar
- 1/2 cup chopped walnuts or pecans
- 2 tablespoons all-purpose flour
- 2 tablespoons unsalted butter, melted
- 1 teaspoon ground cinnamon, or more to taste

MAKING THE STREUSEL: In a small bowl, mix all the streusel ingredients together with a fork.

PREPARING THE APRICOTS, IF USING: For *fresh apricots*, pit and cut them into small pieces. Add to a small saucepan along with the sugar, orange zest, and juice. Cook over medium-high heat, stirring with a wooden spoon, until the consistency of marmalade. This should take 10 to 15 minutes, but watch carefully because you don't want to scorch the pot. Set aside. If using *dried apricots*, cut them up into smallish pieces and cook as above with the sugar, zest, and juice until the dried apricot pieces are plumped, 5 to 10 minutes. (The raisins get added later on in the recipe.)

MAKING THE CAKE: Preheat your oven to 375°. Grease and flour an 8-inch square baking pan or an 8-inch round springform pan. In an ample bowl, mix flour, sugar, baking

APRICOT VARIATION
(OPTIONAL)

- 3 *large fresh apricots, or*
  1/2 cup dried apricots
- 1/3 *cup granulated white*
  sugar
- *Grated zest and juice*
  from 1 orange (about
  1 teaspoon grated zest
  and 1/4 cup juice)
- 1/3 *cup raisins*

CAKE

- 1 1/2 *cups all-purpose flour*
- 3/4 *cup granulated white*
  sugar
- 1 *tablespoon baking powder*
- 1/4 *teaspoon salt*
- 1/4 *cup solid vegetable*
  shortening
- 2 *large eggs*
- 1/2 *cup milk*
- 1 *teaspoon vanilla extract*

powder, and salt. With pastry blender or two knives held like a scissors, cut in shortening until mixture looks like bread crumbs.

In a separate bowl, beat together the eggs, milk, and vanilla.

Stir the milk mixture into the flour mixture just until the dry ingredients are evenly moistened.

IF DOING THE APRICOT VARIATION: Spread the apricot mixture, fresh or dried, over the bottom of the prepared baking pan, and scatter the raisins over the top. With a rubber spatula, spread half the batter over the apricot mixture in the pan. Sprinkle half the streusel mix over the batter. Add the other half of the batter, spreading evenly, and sprinkle the remaining streusel on top. If not using the apricot mixture, then just layer on the batter and streusel mixture in the same way.

Bake in the 375° oven 40 to 45 minutes, until a wooden pick inserted in center comes out clean. Let the cake cool in the pan on a wire rack for 15 minutes. Turn the coffee cake out from the baking pan onto the rack or remove the sides of the springform pan and let the cake cool further.

Serve the coffee cake warm or at room temperature—a wonderful accompaniment to breakfast eggs or fruit, or by itself with freshly brewed coffee. A small piece has been known to find its way into the field.

MAKES 10 TO 12 SLICES, OR EVEN A FEW MORE IF FEEDING A LARGE CROWD FOR BREAKFAST OR TEA

Pain à Paree

Oh, let's not pretend: This is a form of French toast! But French toast on a different order of experience from what you've had. French toast was originally *Pain Perdu* (lost bread)—stale bread, dipped in egg batter and fried to bring it back to life. Feather Rolls (page 32) or Hot Cross Buns (page 22) that have gone stale (Mrs. Hogget's don't last that long) make terrific French toast: Slice them vertically into three slices and dip. Or use any bread that is past the prime of life, cut into rounds or triangles. For garnish, Esme often uses pie cherries, cinnamon-sugar, applesauce flavored with allspice, or a scattering of fresh berries. If you want to have this ready first thing in the morning, you can soak the bread overnight.

2 tablespoons unsalted
  butter, for the pan
1 baguette French bread
  (or any loaf will do)
4 large eggs, lightly beaten
1/2 cup milk
1/2 cup orange juice
1/2 teaspoon vanilla extract
1/8 teaspoon salt

Spread a 15 × 10-inch jelly-roll pan with the butter. Cut the French bread into 1-inch-thick diagonal slices.

In a bowl, beat the eggs. Then whisk in the milk, orange juice, vanilla, and salt, making a batter. Dip both sides of the French bread slices into the batter, then lay them out on the jelly-roll pan, cover with plastic wrap, and refrigerate for 4 hours or overnight.

When ready to bake, preheat your oven to 375°. Place the jelly-roll pan with the bread in the oven, and bake for 12 minutes on the first side. Turn them over, and bake 10 to 12 minutes, until bread is puffy and golden brown.

Top with a swirl of sweet butter and a generous drizzle of maple syrup.

MAKES 6 TO 8 HELPINGS

Best-of-Show Popovers

The simplest, most delicate breakfast cakes they've ever had—that's what bake-off judges say about Esme Hoggett's popovers. Arthur Hoggett just smiles—"Righty-o"—and reaches for the marmalade. Popovers—called such because they bake in a hot oven, puff up with expanding steam, dome, and spill over the top of the cups—are made with no leavening; it's the eggs that do it. Some cooks make dill-Parmesan popovers, or whole wheat, or Cheddar cheese, or other variations. But it's the simple, unadorned popover for the purist Hoggetts. Well, except, occasionally . . . "Buttermilk! Very good," Esme says. "Light, a wee bit custardy inside. I don't mind a nice buttermilk popover." (Just substitute buttermilk for the plain milk, she says, and add a teaspoon of light-brown sugar.) In this recipe, Esme begins with her farm kitchen-tested method—a cold oven rather than a preheated one.

2 *large eggs*
1 *cup all-purpose flour*
1/2 *teaspoon salt*
1 *cup milk*

Break the eggs into a pitcher or lipped bowl so the batter will be easy to pour into the custard cups.

Sift together the flour with the salt onto a sheet of waxed paper, and then stir it into the eggs along with the milk. Mix well, but not too well—disregard any lumps.

Butter thoroughly 8 standard-size muffin-pan cups or four 6-ounce custard cups. Pour the batter into the cups, dividing equally. Place the cups on a baking sheet for easy handling, and put in a cold oven.

Turn the oven to 425° and bake 35 to 40 minutes. Do not open the oven door while baking or the popovers will collapse. They are done when they've doubled in size and are golden brown on top.

Serve them piping hot with sweet butter or fresh fruit preserves for a golden morning delicacy. Esme sometimes serves them for lunch, stuffed with her curried egg salad or a nice feta cheese-tomato salad.

MAKES 8 MUFFIN-SIZE OR 4 CUSTARD CUP-SIZE POPOVERS

Buttermilk-Apple Wheat Cakes

"Hoggett dear," Mrs. Hoggett asked brightly one frosty morn, "how are my apple hotcakes like *opossums*?" She held the serving plate aloft, waiting. Hoggett gave her a frosty look. "Well, let me tell you then," she prattled cheerfully, giving him a stack of three for starters. "The pancake, like the opossum, comes to us practically unchanged almost from the dinosaur era. What do you think of that?!" "Oh," Hoggett said. Whereupon they both fell on their buttermilk-apple wheat cakes and devoured them. As always when it comes to food, Mrs. Hoggett knew her stuff. Pancakes, one of the earliest forms of bread, started out as ground-meal-and-water patties slapped on a hot rock, and since then have been found in nearly every culture in every age, as appetizers, main dishes with stuffings, and desserts. In this pancake, the slightly sour buttermilk plays enticingly off the sweet apple and hint of honey in the batter. You can substitute nectarines, peaches, blueberries, huckleberries, blackberries—whatever is ripe and in abundance in the orchard or in the berry patches along the stream. For a special treat, sauté extra diced fruit in a little butter, and tumble over the stack of cakes, along with a drizzle of syrup.

(continued)

2 cups buttermilk, at room
  temperature
3 large eggs
2 tablespoons honey
2 tablespoons vegetable oil
2 cups whole-wheat flour
2 tablespoons wheat germ
2 teaspoons baking soda
1 teaspoon salt
2 cups diced red apples (about
  2 medium-size apples, with
  or without skins)
Butter, for the griddle

In an ample bowl, stir together the buttermilk, eggs, honey, and oil until very well blended.

In another bowl, stir together the flour, wheat germ, baking soda, and salt. Stir the buttermilk mixture into the flour mixture just until evenly moistened; don't overmix. Better to have a few harmless lumps rather than coarse pancakes resulting from overbeating. Fold in the apple.

Preheat your griddle to medium hot, so a drop of water sizzles and dances. Lightly butter the griddle and pour a small ladleful of batter on for each pancake. Cook until golden-brown on the bottom with bubbles beginning to break on top, about 3 to 4 minutes. Then flip over and cook until golden brown on the bottom, another 2 or 3 minutes. These may take longer to cook than plain pancakes, but it's worth the wait.

Serve with butter and maple syrup, or one of Esme's Flavored Whipped Butters (see page 138)—a three-star breakfast for the famished.

MAKES ABOUT 12 PANCAKES (OF AVERAGE SIZE—NOT HUGE)

Feather Rolls

These are yeast breads, and as such, have to be allowed a little time to rise—can't rush these. They end up as high and light as their name implies and are the perfect all-purpose roll. They go well with almost any meal, any food. Out of the corner of her eye, Esme has spotted Farmer Hoggett walking out the door with several of these rolls hidden behind his leg, for a certain sheep-pig. "Have you ever seen a pig swoon?" Esme asks. " Such a sight!" Kids or work crew love them too as sandwich bread the next day.

1/2 cup milk

1/2 cup plus 1 teaspoon granulated white sugar

1/2 cup (1 stick) unsalted butter

1 teaspoon salt

1/4 cup warm water (105° to 115°)

2 envelopes active dry yeast

2 large eggs, lightly beaten

4 cups all-purpose flour

In a heavy saucepan, heat the milk until small bubbles appear around the edge—this is called scalding, and helps to retard the souring of milk, which is less a concern these days with modern refrigeration. Stir in the 1/2 cup sugar, butter, and salt, and keep on stirring to melt the butter and dissolve the sugar. Remove from heat and cool to lukewarm.

In an ample bowl, stir together the 1 teaspoon sugar and the warm water. Sprinkle the yeast over the top and let it stand until the mixture gets foamy, 5 or 10 minutes. (If the yeast doesn't foam, then you know your yeast is no longer active, and the rolls won't rise. Best to get another packet—check the expiration date.) Then stir to dissolve the yeast.

Add the milk mixture to the yeast mixture, and then the beaten eggs, mixing well. Add the flour gradually, beating vigorously until you have a soft, smooth dough. Turn the dough into a lightly buttered bowl, cover with a clean dish towel, and let rise in a warm place until doubled in size, about 2 hours.

Punch the dough down and turn out onto a lightly floured board. Knead lightly several times. Divide the dough in half.

MAKING THE ROLLS: Roll one half of the dough into a 12-inch-long rope, and cut into twelve 1-inch pieces. Butter 12 standard-size muffin-pan cups, and place a piece of dough in each one. To make cloverleaf rolls, divide each piece into thirds. Roll each third into a ball, and place 3 balls in each muffin-pan cup. Repeat this whole thing with the other half of the dough and another 12 muffin-pan cups, for a total of 24 rolls.

OR, FOR MAKING WEDGES: Roll or pat out half of the dough into an 8-inch circle, place on a buttered baking sheet, and cut with a sharp knife into 8 equal wedges, keeping the wedges in the shape of the circle. Repeat with other half of dough on another baking sheet for a total of 16 wedges.

Whether making rolls or wedges, cover with a clean dish towel, and let rise in a warm place until doubled in size, about 30 minutes.

When ready to bake, preheat your oven to 350°. Then bake, about 15 minutes for the rolls, or about 20 minutes for the wedges, or until tops are golden brown and a wooden pick inserted in the middle comes out clean.

Serve warm or at room temperature, as an all-purpose dinner roll. Perfect for pushing gravy around on a plate.

MAKES 24 ROLLS OR 16 WEDGES

Bishop's Bread

Originally, this was for Sundays and holidays when the Bishop himself might come to dinner. "Well, you never know, do you?" Esme says. The bread, almost like a chocolate fruitcake, is such a treat that Mrs. Hoggett makes up her own holidays several times a year just to have an excuse to make it (and faithfully sets an extra place for the Bishop). Amazingly, the Bishop's piece never goes begging.

2 1/2 cups all-purpose flour
1 tablespoon baking powder
1 teaspoon salt
4 ounces German sweet baking chocolate
2 cups finely chopped pecans
1 cup chopped dates
1 cup chopped maraschino cherries, well drained
4 large eggs
1 1/4 cups granulated white sugar

Preheat your oven to 325°. Butter a 9 × 5 × 3-inch loaf pan.

In an ample bowl, stir together the flour, baking powder, and salt. Cut the chocolate into small pieces and add it along with the pecans, dates, and cherries to the flour mixture. Stir to coat the chocolate pieces very thoroughly with the flour.

In another bowl, with an electric mixer, beat the eggs until foamy. Add the sugar gradually and continue beating until the eggs are thick and lemon-colored, about 4 minutes. Be patient. Fold in the fruit-nut-chocolate mixture, blending well. Pour the batter into the prepared loaf pan.

Bake in the 325° oven for about 1 1/2 hours. The top should be brown and a wooden pick inserted in the center should come out clean. Cool the bread in the pan on a wire rack for 10 minutes. Turn the bread out onto the rack to cool.

Serve warm or at room temperature, plain or with sweet butter. And wrap a piece to take to your favorite neighbor.

MAKES 1 LOAF, 10 TO 12 SLICES (AND SAVE A SLICE FOR THE BISHOP)

Soups to Nourish the Body and Warm the Soul

"A meat stock?! Never, ever."

Substantial soups are a mainstay of Mrs. Hoggett's cooking—from sturdy cups of creamy Cheddar-cauliflower soup and steaming bowls of minestrone to a simmering kettle of sweet and sour beet soup.

At midday dinner, evening supper, and late-night meals when the harvest crew works into the dark, or even at breakfast, hearty, delicious soups are on Mrs. Hoggett's menu. "Quick nourishment for famished farmhands," she says. "Food that warms their souls." And of all farm food, soups may be the most savory and varied, thanks to the farm cook's love affair with fresh garden vegetables. We forget that when vegetables don't have to travel farther than the few steps from the kitchen garden to the kitchen table, they have extravagant flavor which translates directly into *unforgettable* soups. And that flavor is aided, to be sure, by a farm cook's devotion to the herb garden: thyme, rosemary, chives, basil, dill, and fennel, all located just beyond the back door. Nothing like fresh herbs to gloriously complicate the flavors of the soup pot.

"The crucial meat stock?" Mrs. Hoggett says, "A lovely old sacred cow, gone to the pasture in the sky. A myth! thank you very much." Esme's own Savory Vegetable Stock helps keep it there. It will deepen the flavors and add body to every soup that calls for a stock. Here too are Wild Mushroom Soup, a classic minestrone, Roasted Garlic Soup, a cool cucumber with chopped walnuts, smooth cream of fennel, French onion soup with roquefort, Tomato-Parmesan-Lentil Soup, a lemony pistou, and more. Make sure there's always a burner free at the back of the stove for the soup pot.

Savory Vegetable Stock

This versatile all-season soup stock from the Hoggett Farm kitchen garden is a delicious foundation broth that can be elaborated on with seasonal vegetables and herbs. And it makes a fast, flavorful, just-about-ready-made soup by itself with the addition of white beans or rice, some seasonings, and a little simmering. The stock is useful elsewhere in cooking, too—for example, adding dimension to risotto and other dishes that call for something more than just water.

"Now, you do know that your stockpot is a good place for some vegetables, and not others," Esme says, "for some leftovers or parings, but not all. It is *not* a recycling pail to pop your old or spoiled vegetables into—oh my, no." Avoid the cabbage family, for example—broccoli, cauliflower, Brussels sprouts. No turnips. "And don't overuse greens—two or three cups is plenty." Potato parings, corn cobs, and basil and marjoram stems are fine to use, but not onion skins or artichoke leavings. "Babe—now, he's a different story," Esme says. "Pigs are omnivores, oh yes they are. Babe *is* a recycling pot. And so appreciative. Stems, leftovers, all those other ingredients you don't want in your stock kettle—Babe hors d'oeuvres!"

3 tablespoons olive oil

4 onions, chopped

2 leeks (just the white part), trimmed, rinsed well, and chopped

3 ribs celery, trimmed and chopped

8 silver-dollar-size fresh mushrooms, the white button variety, trimmed, wiped clean, and sliced

In a stockpot, heat the oil over medium heat—make sure the pot is large enough to hold the 2 gallons of water and all the ingredients. Add the onions, cover the pot, and cook over medium heat until onions are translucent and softened, about 10 minutes. This is a technique aptly called "sweating," because liquid oozes out of the vegetables as they cook.

Add the leeks, celery, mushrooms, and carrots, and sweat them, covered, until tender, another 10 minutes or so.

Add the water, lentils, garlic, salt, pepper, and the bouquet garni. Turn the heat to high and bring to a boil. Then reduce

3 carrots, trimmed and
  chopped
2 gallons cold water
1/4 cup dried lentils
6 cloves garlic, peeled
1 tablespoon salt
8 twists freshly ground black
  pepper

BOUQUET GARNI
  Fresh thyme, sage, marjoram,
  a bay leaf, and parsley
  sprigs, all tied up in a
  bundle or in a piece of
  cheesecloth—easily
  removed from the stock
  after it has simmered

the heat, and simmer, uncovered, for 1 hour. From time to time, with a large spoon, skim off any foam that gathers on the surface, and discard. Cooking the vegetables much more than an hour is pointless—they've yielded their flavors by then.

Strain the stock immediately through a fine sieve—don't let the ingredients sit in the liquid. And now, if you choose, boil down the liquid further, uncovered, to concentrate flavors.

Let the stock cool, then chill. To speed up the cooling, pour the stock into smaller containers. Skim off any layer of accumulated material that rises to the surface. Store in the refrigerator for up to a week, and boil before using. Or freeze in ice cube trays or 1-cup amounts for up to 6 months.

MAKES ABOUT 2 QUARTS

M. Mande's Onion Soup with Crumbled Roquefort

This is a two-hundred-year-old French farm recipe sent to Babe from a sheep-farming admirer, M. Claude Mande, in the Roquefort region of south-central France. Authentic *Soupe à l'Oignon Française* can be made with other blue-veined cheeses—Italian Gorgonzola, English Stilton, Danish Blue. And it can be made without the Armagnac or brandy. But Babe, a pig of precision in all his endeavors, prefers to see this made as prescribed. Yes, he gets his own bowl when Mrs. Hoggett makes it—"Hooo-eeee! Come Pig!"—and he relishes the sharp tingle of Roquefort in his nose when he eats it. A rare treat for a pig, and for all other guests at the Hoggett table. You'll need four ovenproof soup bowls so you can brown the cheese at the end.

1/4 cup olive oil

1 large or 2 medium-size onions, thinly sliced

1 cup crumbled Roquefort cheese (about 6 ounces)

2 tablespoons all-purpose flour

4 cups water

1/3 cup heavy cream

1/2 teaspoon salt

1/4 teaspoon freshly ground white pepper

1 small baguette

4 teaspoons Armagnac or brandy

1 1/2 cups shredded Gruyère cheese (about 6 ounces)

In a soup kettle or large saucepan, heat the oil over medium heat. Add the onions, and sauté, stirring occasionally, until caramelized—deep golden brown—about 35 minutes. Watch carefully so the onions don't get too dark. Add half the Roquefort cheese and the 2 tablespoons flour. Cook, stirring constantly, for 1 minute.

Stir in the water and cream. Season with the salt and pepper. Bring to a boil. Reduce the heat to a simmer and cook, uncovered, for 25 to 30 minutes.

Thinly slice the baguette into 12 slices. Place on a baking sheet and toast in a preheated 450° oven, 5 minutes.

Preheat the broiler.

Ladle the soup into 4 ovenproof bowls. Spoon a teaspoon of Armagnac onto the surface of the soup in each bowl, and cover with the toasted bread. Sprinkle the toast with the shredded Gruyère and the remaining crumbled Roquefort. Slide the soup bowls under the broiler until a bubbly, golden brown crust forms, 2 to 3 minutes. Keep a watchful eye.

Serve immediately, with a nice white wine and a green salad with pears dressed in a champagne vinaigrette. Heaven!

MAKES 4 SERVINGS

Kelly Sims's Roasted Garlic Soup

The smell of this dish makes Esme Hoggett want to lock herself in a dust-proof room and write a long novel in search of her past. As a child, she went to a one-room country school—grades one through eight combined, one teacher, and twelve pupils, all of them related. No plumbing or electricity, no insulation, and the only heat in winter coming from the cast-iron coal stove in the middle of the room. The littlest kids got to sit closest to the stove. One luxury they did have was hot lunch. On top of the stove sat a big flat pan of water. Every morning each child would place his or her lunch—brought in a quart jar—in the hot water, and all morning it would heat up. At lunchtime they would have a nice hot meal, usually leftovers from the night before—soups, stews, chili, casseroles. When Kelly Sims brought his mother's garlic soup, everybody would soon know it, as the aroma, despite the sealed lid, permeated the classroom. That smell haunted Esme into adulthood—was it the crush she'd had on little towheaded Kelly, or was it the soup? Finally she paid a visit to old Mrs. Sims and got the recipe, and now she cooks it when feeling nostalgic. "It's a lovely pure concoction, and quite mild," she says.

(continued)

"The roasting takes the harsh edge off the garlic. Oh my, yes, it does take me back. And another good thing—you don't have to peel your garlic to make it. Isn't that grand?"

3 heads garlic (*not cloves—heads, whole and unpeeled*)

2 tablespoons olive oil

1 large onion, sliced

1 leek (*just the white part*), trimmed, rinsed well, and sliced

2 large russet potatoes, peeled and sliced

2 quarts water

GARLIC "CHIPS"

3 or 4 cloves elephant garlic (*these are the huge cloves*)

2 tablespoons olive oil

1 red bell pepper, for garnish

1 cup heavy cream

1/2 teaspoon salt, or to taste

1/4 teaspoon freshly ground black pepper

Preheat your oven to 350°. Roast the whole, unpeeled heads of garlic on a baking sheet in the oven for 45 minutes. While the papery skin will turn dark brown, the pulp will become soft and golden brown. When cool enough to handle, slip off the skins. Slice the garlic heads and reserve.

In a large soup kettle or saucepan, heat the 2 tablespoons oil. Add the onion and leek, and sauté until soft but not brown, about 8 minutes. Add the sliced roasted garlic heads, the sliced potatoes, and the water. Simmer, partially covered, for 1 hour.

MAKING GARLIC "CHIPS": Peel and thinly slice the elephant garlic. In a small skillet, heat the 2 tablespoons oil. Add the garlic slices, and sauté until they become golden brown garlic "chips," about 2 minutes. Transfer with a slotted spoon to paper towels to drain, and reserve.

Core and seed bell pepper. Cut into thin strips, and reserve.

Just before the soup is done, stir in the cream. In batches, puree the soup in a blender or food processor, and then strain through a sieve into a bowl for extra smoothness. Season with the salt and pepper. If need be, reheat the soup, but don't let it come to a boil.

Pour into 8 bowls, and garnish with the garlic "chips" and red bell pepper strips.

Serve with a freshly baked, crusty baguette and some soft, runny cheese, or a cool green avocado and tomato salad.

MAKES 8 SERVINGS

Cauliflower Soup with Aged White Cheddar and Toasted Caraway

"Painters and poets have leave to lie," Mrs. H. says, "but not cheeses!" She's talking about the sharp, orangey Cheddars for sale in stores. "Don't be fooled. The color doesn't mean they're richer, they're just dyed, that's all. What do you think of that?" For this soup she recommends a not-too-strong, aged white Vermont cheddar. It's deep and flavorful, but won't overpower the delicate cauliflower and nutty roasted caraway flavors. "This is a perfect winter soup," says Mrs. H., who adores a year-round vegetable. "Marry it to a nice Cheddar, and there you have a happy family." Substitute cousin broccoli or closer cousin broccoflower for a variation on the same soup.

SOUP BASE

- 3 cups cauliflower flowerets (about 2/3 of a small head)
- 3 russet potatoes, scrubbed and coarsely chopped
- 1 carrot, trimmed and chopped
- 1 cup chopped onion
- 3 cloves garlic, chopped
- 1 teaspoon salt
- 3 cups Savory Vegetable Stock (page 36) or canned vegetable broth

MAKING THE SOUP BASE: In a soup kettle or large saucepan, combine the 3 cups of cauliflower flowerets, potatoes, carrot, onion, garlic, salt, and vegetable stock or broth. Bring to a boil. Then cover the pot, reduce the heat to low, and simmer until the potatoes are tender, about 20 minutes. Let cool.

In batches, remove the solids with a large slotted spoon to a blender or food processor, add a little liquid from the pot, and puree. Stir the puree back into the remaining liquid in the pot.

PREPARING THE FLAVORINGS: Heat a skillet over medium heat. Add the caraway seeds and then toast them, shaking the pan occasionally, to bring out the flavors, 3 to 4 minutes. Watch carefully and don't let them burn.

1/2 teaspoon caraway seeds

1 cup shredded aged white
Cheddar cheese, or plain
unaged Cheddar (about
4 ounces)

1/2 cup milk

1/4 teaspoon dry mustard

Freshly ground black pepper,
to taste

FINISHING

2 cups additional cauliflower
flowerets

1/2 cup buttermilk, warmed

1 scallion, finely chopped

Shredded Cheddar

Paprika, for garnish

Place the soup over low heat. Stir in all the ingredients listed under "Flavorings." Heat gently, but do not let the soup boil.

PREPARE THE FINISHING: In a saucepan with an inch of water, steam the 2 cups of cauliflower flowerets, covered, just until tender, 3 to 4 minutes. Drain and add these to the soup.

Stir the buttermilk into the soup just before serving. Ladle into 6 soup bowls. Serve immediately, topped with the chopped scallion, extra cheese, and a sprinkle of paprika.

Sautéed elephant Garlic "Chips" are a nice crunchy accompaniment (see page 40), along with a salad of strong greens and sun-dried tomatoes.

MAKES 6 SERVINGS

Thick Tomato Soup with Fresh Sorrel

"This is the very essence of soup," Esme Hoggett says. "Hardy, warming, comforting." With its thickness, soft texture, and sweet fresh tomato flavor, it provides equal parts succor and sustenance. "It's the kind of soup that makes you feel quite safe," Mrs. H. says, "whether you're a frazzled grown-up or an exhausted little one. Children? Yes, indeed. They adore this soup." You can make it as thick and filling as you like by the addition of more bread. Use challah, the traditional Sabbath bread of the Jews, or any

(continued)

soft Mediterranean-style bread. The ripe tomato flavor is given a nice zesty lemony turn by the French sorrel, which is especially plentiful in spring. The soup is just as good the second day, if you're lucky enough to have any leftovers. "Better!" Esme says. "You don't have to cook!"

3 tablespoons olive oil

1 medium-size onion, chopped

1 green bell pepper, cored, seeded, and diced

20 cloves garlic, peeled and thinly sliced (that's right, 20—the garlic flavor sweetens as the soup cooks)

12 ripe tomatoes (about 4 1/2 pounds), peeled (page 114) and sliced

2 cups Savory Vegetable Stock (page 36) or water

1 bay leaf

12 fresh sorrel leaves, stemmed and cut into thin strips

4 to 6 thick slices soft-texture bread, cubed

1 teaspoon salt

Parmesan cheese, for garnish, shaved or grated

In a large soup pot, heat the oil over medium heat. Add the onion and green pepper and sauté until tender, 5 to 6 minutes. Add the sliced garlic, tomatoes, vegetable stock or water, bay leaf, and sorrel (saving a few pretty strands for later). Bring to a vigorous bubble, then reduce the heat and simmer, uncovered, for 30 minutes.

Add the cubes of bread for the desired consistency— remember, the more bread the thicker the soup. Add the salt. Simmer until the bread is softened, another 5 to 10 minutes. Don't forget to remove the bay leaf.

Ladle into bowls and serve immediately, with a garnish of bright sorrel ribbons and Parmesan cheese.

You can never get enough of a good thing, such as garlic—so serve this soup with garlic bread, plus roasted potatoes and a hot or cold green bean salad.

MAKES ABOUT 8 SERVINGS

Great White Northern Minestrone

This recipe originally called for *salt pork*! "Well, not on your life!" Mrs. Hoggett says. "Can you imagine?" Alas, not everyone cherishes pigs as the Hoggetts have come to. Thank heaven there are perfectly good substitutes—ingredients that provide the same meaty, smoky flavor. Try smoked dried chipotle peppers or smoked mozzarella cheese. Both will do the trick. "Why, I would use them in baked beans, too, if I were you," Mrs. H. says, "if you do see what I mean. *Please.*" (See other meat-substitute ideas in

(continued)

Tomato-Parmesan-Lentil Soup, page 54.) This satisfying white bean-and-rice soup is very much a meal in itself. The rice adds extra body *and* soaks up broth, especially if the soup sits for a day or so in your refrigerator—so scatter in the rice sparingly, if you're planning on leftovers.

1 quart water

1/2 cup dried Great Northern white beans

1/4 cup olive oil

1 cup fresh green peas (or frozen, if need be)

1 medium-size unpeeled zucchini, trimmed and diced

3 medium-size carrots, trimmed and diced

1 medium-size potato (you can leave the skin on if you like), diced

1 rib celery, diced

2 tablespoons chopped onion

1/2 cup chopped leek (white part of 1 to 2 leeks), rinsed well

2 cups chopped tomatoes (2 medium-size)

2 tablespoons tomato paste

In a saucepan, bring the 1 quart of water to a boil. Add the dried white beans and remove the pan from the heat. Let soak for 1 hour. Then simmer, uncovered, for 1 1/2 hours. Keep a sharp eye toward the end of the cooking, to make sure there is a little water left in the pan so there's no scorching.

In a large skillet, heat 2 tablespoons of the olive oil over medium heat. Add the peas, zucchini, carrots, potato, and celery, and cook for 2 to 3 minutes, stirring with a wooden spoon. Remove from the heat.

In a large soup kettle, heat the remaining 2 tablespoons of olive oil over medium heat. Add the onion and leek, and cook until light brown, about 5 minutes. Stir in the chopped tomatoes, the vegetables from the skillet, the tomato paste, the stock or water, bay leaf, and salt and pepper.

Simmer, uncovered, for 25 minutes. Discard the bay leaf. Drain the white beans, and add along with the rice and parsley. Simmer, uncovered, 20 minutes longer or just until rice is done.

2 quarts Savory Vegetable Stock (page 36), canned vegetable broth, or water

1 bay leaf

1/2 teaspoon salt, or to taste

1/4 teaspoon freshly ground black pepper, or to taste

1/2 cup raw rice

2 parsley sprigs, chopped

2 ounces smoked dried chipotle peppers, soaked in hot water to plump, and then seeded and chopped, or smoked mozzarella cheese, diced, for garnish

Parmesan cheese, thinly shaved, for garnish

Ladle into bowls and garnish with chopped chipotle peppers or diced mozzarella. Serve steaming hot, with a bowl of Parmesan shavings on the table.

Irresistible with this are crostini (small toast rounds) topped with blue cheese and chopped toasted walnuts. On the farm, you can never have enough cheese.

MAKES 6 TO 8 SERVINGS

Cousin Dick's Smooth Cream of Fennel Soup

A little red MG convertible spun into the driveway. "Cornsilk Boyd," Arthur Hoggett announced. "Here for dinner." The black sheep of Esme's family. He waved amiably, a bushy-mustached man with an easy grin. Dick Boyd, Esme's second cousin once-removed, had been just another twinkly-eyed roughneck kid until one escapade branded him—the time he talked Esme and other trusting youths in their one-room school into trying to learn how to smoke. With corn silk, toilet paper for wrapping, and wooden matches filched from the school stove, Dick got them all lighted up behind the schoolhouse. Choking, spitting, eyes watering—such a sight! And before they knew it, the grass caught fire, and the boys' outhouse burned down. Quick-witted Dick led the kids in running a quarter mile to the nearest farmhouse for water, and in the end they saved the schoolhouse itself. Dick was a hero, of sorts. But "Cornsilk" Boyd was a closely-watched train thereafter. He grew up to run a successful car-paint distributorship and was elected township selectman year after year. People still watched him; watched that twinkle in his eye as he tried to talk them into doing things. Today it was a recipe for Cousin Esme: creamy fennel soup from Farmer Frank over in Phoenix County. "You've *got* to try it," Dick said. "Big, rich. Yet so darn subtle." Esme raised a brow. "Well, we'll just see about that, won't we?" She took the recipe straight into the kitchen.

1/4 cup (1/2 stick) unsalted
   butter, or olive oil
1 medium-size onion, thinly
   sliced
3 large fennel bulbs (about
   3 1/2 pounds)*

In a soup kettle or large saucepan, heat the butter or olive oil over medium heat. Add the onion, and sauté until it just begins to brown, about 5 minutes.

Meanwhile, trim off the stems from the fennel bulbs, and then thinly slice the bulbs. (Save a few leafy green tops for garnish.) Add the sliced fennel to the pot, and sauté along with the onion until the fennel is slightly tender and

1 1/2 teaspoons salt
1/4 teaspoon freshly ground
    white pepper
About 4 cups water, as needed
3/4 cup heavy cream (or less
    if desired)
Splash of Pernod (a delicious
    licorice-flavored liqueur,
    optional)

translucent, about 15 minutes. Season with the salt and white pepper.

Add water to the pot so the vegetables are covered by about 1 inch, about 4 cups.

Stir in the cream, cover, and bring to a boil. Then reduce the heat to a simmer and cook, partially covered, for 30 minutes, or until everything is thoroughly tender.

In batches, remove the solids with a big slotted spoon from the pot and place in a blender or food processor, add a little liquid from the pot, and puree. Strain the puree through a sieve back into the liquid in the pot, and stir to combine. Taste for the seasoning, and add a splash of Pernod, if you wish, to bring the anise or licorice flavor of the fennel to a peak.

Ladle into 6 warm bowls, top with a garnish of pretty fennel greens, and serve immediately.

Surround each steaming bowl with toast points spread with Boursault cheese or sweet butter.

*NOTE: You can substitute either celery or asparagus for the fennel in this wonderfully simple but satisfying soup. Just leave out the Pernod.

MAKES 6 SERVINGS

Sweet Carrot Soup with Basil

In Arthur Hoggett's youth, this was a soup the children in his family especially fancied. It was a Sunday soup—for the trip to church that they never missed. In winter, snow runners replaced the wheels on the two big farm wagons, and two families would ride in the beds of the wagons the four-and-a-half miles to Sunday services—two long hours each way in the piercing sub-zero wind. But there were comforts. One was the soapstones—big limestone slabs—which sat all night on the top of the stoves heating up, then went into the sleigh-wagons. The families huddled, heads and all, underneath big woolen blankets, gossiping and passing the time, their feet toasty on the soapstones, while Hoggett's father and his uncle drove the teams of horses. The children had another comfort—hot soup in thermoses, and Hoggett's mother's sweet carrot soup with its touches of orange juice and honey was the hands-down favorite.

When serving this simple-to-make soup at the table, Mrs. H. varies its complexion with garnishes: long thin strips of fresh mint in place of the basil, or a splash of sherry mixed in at the last minute. A zigzag of crème fraîche across the surface of each bowl gives it one twist, a sprinkle of fresh-grated apple with a dash of cinnamon, another.

3 tablespoons olive oil

6 to 7 large carrots, trimmed, peeled, and thinly sliced

1 large onion, thinly sliced

3 teaspoons honey

1 teaspoon chopped fresh thyme, or 1/2 teaspoon dried

4 cups Savory Vegetable Stock (page 36), canned vegetable broth, or water

In a soup kettle, heat the oil over medium heat. Add the carrots and onion, and sauté, stirring occasionally, until tender, about 20 minutes. Add the honey and thyme, and cook for about a minute, stirring until blended.

Add the stock and bring the soup to a boil. Reduce to a healthy simmer, and cook, partially covered, for 30 minutes.

In batches, remove the solids with a big slotted spoon to a blender or food processor, add a little liquid from the pot, and puree. Stir the puree back into the liquid in the pot.

(continued)

"Sweet Dani" Pistou
and Sweet Carrot Soup with Basil

1/4 cup orange juice
1/2 teaspoon fresh lemon juice
Freshly ground black pepper,
    to taste
1 bunch fresh sweet basil,
    cut into long thin strips

Over low heat, stir in the orange juice and lemon juice. Season with pepper to taste.

Ladle into bowls and garnish with the strips of fresh sweet basil.

Serve with fresh rye bread or challah and a bitter green salad—escarole, endive, or chicory.

MAKES 4 SERVINGS

"Sweet Dani" Pistou

The week the annual seed catalogues arrive presages big things at Hoggett Farm—a frenzy of activity in Esme's herb and vegetable gardens. This last season birthed a new star. "Indeed! Oh my!" Mrs. H. said, proudly displaying her riot of leafing basil plants. "'Sweet Dani.' Pretty as anything in my flower garden!" She got right down there with her nostrils—pinching, rubbing, sniffing. "Strong, lemony . . . beguiling! That's the very word, isn't it? Hmm. High in *essential oils*, I'd say, and hmm, yes, *citral content*. Beguiling—wouldn't you agree?" Babe, treading the rows nearby, found it actually a bit *stifling*, but he would never think of letting on. Esme plucked a big handful of the lemony basil leaves and plunged her face into them, drinking the bouquet. "Such vigor! Their destiny—now, that would be—why, a glorious pistou!" She rose up from the waving greens. "Hoggett! Come and give a smell! Oh, this'll do nicely." And indeed it does, lending her classic Mediterranean-style pesto soup a dramatic *enrichissement* of aroma and flavor.

PESTO

2 cups "Sweet Dani" basil
(or your own favorite
variety), loosely packed

6 walnut halves, or
3 tablespoons chopped

5 cloves garlic, peeled

1/3 cup extra-virgin olive oil
or regular olive oil

1/4 cup grated Parmesan

SOUP BASE

2 quarts Savory Vegetable
Stock (page 36), canned
vegetable broth, or water

1 1/2 cups chopped leeks, rinsed

3 carrots, trimmed and diced

2 potatoes, diced

1 teaspoon salt

1/2 teaspoon freshly ground
black pepper

1 cup fresh green peas (or
frozen peas if you must)

1 cup fresh green beans

1 slice stale bread, crumbed

1 can (15 ounces) kidney
beans, drained and rinsed

1 cup vermicelli pasta,
broken into pieces

MAKING THE PESTO: In a food processor, process the basil leaves, walnuts, and garlic until finely chopped. Then, with the processor running, add the oil in a thread until well blended. Add the Parmesan and process until blended. Pour into a large soup tureen and reserve in a warm place.

MAKING THE SOUP BASE: Pour the vegetable stock or water into a soup kettle or large saucepan. Add the leeks, carrots, potatoes, salt, and pepper and bring to a boil. Reduce the heat to a simmer and cook, partially covered, for 30 to 40 minutes, stirring occasionally, or until the vegetables are tender.

Add the peas and green beans, and stir in the stale bread crumbs. Simmer, uncovered, for 10 to 15 minutes, or until the peas and green beans are tender. Add the kidney beans and the vermicelli, and simmer until heated through and the vermicelli is tender, about 10 more minutes.

Add a cup or so of the soup base to the basil mixture in the soup tureen, and stir together well. Gradually add in the rest of the soup, stirring. Ladle into soup bowls immediately. Serve hot.

Garnish with garlic or rosemary croutons. This goes well with thick country bread, a mild creamy goat cheese, and a cool cucumber salad.

MAKES 4 TO 6 SERVINGS

Tomato-Parmesan-Lentil Soup

Pre-Babe, Esme Hoggett would have sworn this hardy classic couldn't be made without a nice ham hock, lamb shank, or smoked sausage—without the tasty little shards of meat and smoky flavor in the broth. "Oh my, yes! It was an article of faith," she says. But the morning after Babe won the National Grand Challenge Sheep Dog Trials, she woke up with an irresistible urge to go cold turkey . . . er, cold pig? She went bustling into a "whole foods" store and said, "Tell me everything you know. Show me everything you've got." She came out arms loaded. "Imagine my amazement—lovely animal-friendly ways to make this soup and that stew and the other omelet!" Now her *nouveau* lentil soup uses non-meat "Canadian bacon," diced and sautéed. It has the exact munchy texture needed and provides every bit as much flavor. For meat broth, she uses a vegetarian "chicken" broth—"without a drop of chicken," she says. "Who can tell?" What's more, she found hot dogs, hamburgers, Spanish-style *chorizo* sausages, and a herd of other "meat" products that had never seen the inside of an abattoir, but that even *her* exquisite palate found as flavorful as any of the animal foods.

1 1/2 tablespoons unsalted butter
2 tablespoons olive oil
2 1/2 tablespoons finely chopped onion
2 1/2 tablespoons finely chopped celery
2 1/2 tablespoons finely chopped carrot
1 tablespoon finely chopped garlic

In a soup kettle or large saucepan, heat 1/2 tablespoon of the butter and the olive oil over medium-low heat. Add the onion, and sauté until almost caramelized, about 4 minutes. Add the celery, carrot, and garlic, and sauté over high heat, stirring often, until the garlic is golden but not browned, about 2 minutes.

Add the vegetarian bacon and the tomatoes with their juice (add 1/3 cup water if there isn't much juice), and bring to a gentle boil. Reduce the heat and simmer steadily, uncovered, for 20 minutes, stirring from time to time.

2 slices vegetarian
"Canadian bacon," diced
(1/3 to 1/2 cup)

1 1/2 cups chopped, peeled
(page 114) ripe plum
tomatoes, with their juice

1/2 pound dried French lentils,
if available (they're smaller
and more flavorful than
other lentils) or, if not, the
regular brown dried lentils

4 cups vegetarian "chicken"
broth (visit your health
food store for this one)
or water

1/2 teaspoon salt

1/4 teaspoon freshly ground
black pepper

3 tablespoons grated
Parmesan cheese, plus
extra for garnishing

Wash the lentils in a sieve under cold running water, drain, and stir into the vegetable mixture in the soup kettle. Add the broth, salt, and pepper, and cook, covered, at a gentle simmer until the lentils are tender, about 45 minutes. As the lentils cook, stir occasionally, and add broth or water if your lentils are particularly absorbent.

Right at the end of the simmering, add the remaining tablespoon of butter and whisk in the 3 tablespoons of Parmesan. Taste for the salt and pepper seasoning, adding more if needed.

Ladle into 4 soup bowls and serve hot, with more Parmesan on the side.

A hot, crispy sourdough baguette, buttered, is excellent with this. Plus a French green salad: butter lettuce, sliced radishes, and cucumbers all dressed with a vinaigrette.

MAKES 4 SERVINGS

tomatoes

Sweet and Sour Beet Soup with Crème Fraîche

Bogdanoff was the sourest man in the county. He was Russian—maybe an embittered Romanov, people said. He had rocky soil, acid water, and his chickens wouldn't lay. His asparagus went to fern behind his back and spoiled before he could cut it. He had a mean wife who couldn't cook and refused to learn. She favored sauerkraut and always had cabbage fermenting in a big crock with a board and a rock on it in a warm place behind the stove, so the kitchen stank year round. Bogdanoff was boney and never smiled—drank sulfuric acid in his tea, he did. He came up to Mrs. Hoggett's kitchen door one day, hat in hand as though approaching a shrine. "Yah, you try maybe?" he said, handing her a piece of paper. On it in his labored hand was scrawled a recipe. He held out a sack with one cabbage, three beets, two onions, a tomato. "Righty-oh," Mrs. Hoggett said, unsure of what he had in mind. He turned around and sat down on the stoop and waited. She got the picture. She made him his borscht, improving on his recipe by leagues. She served it to him at the pine supper table with half a loaf of homemade rye bread and some sweet Hoggett butter. As he was eating the soup, dipping the bread, savoring each bite, she put a bottle of cold beer down in front of him. He looked at it. A tear ran down his cheek. He looked up at her, and he smiled. Esme's version of Bogdanoff's borscht follows. You'll smile, too.

2 *medium-size onions,*
2 *medium-size carrots*
1/4 *small head cabbage*
2 *cloves garlic*
1 *pound fresh beets*
2 *pounds ripe tomatoes*
3 *tablespoons olive oil*
1/4 *cup tomato paste*

Chop the onions. Trim the carrots and thinly slice. Shred the cabbage. Finely chop the garlic. Peel and dice the beets. Peel (page 114), seed, and chop the tomatoes (or chop them whole, if you don't mind the skin and seeds).

In a large soup kettle or pot, heat the olive oil over medium heat. Add the onions, carrots, and cabbage, and cook, covered (this is called sweating, since the vegetables give up

(continued)

1 1/4 quarts Savory Vegetable
    Stock (*page 36*), *canned*
    vegetable broth, or water
  2 teaspoons salt, or
    1 teaspoon if using
    canned broth
Freshly ground black pepper,
    to taste
  1 tablespoon rice or cider
    vinegar
  1 tablespoon honey
  2 teaspoons fresh lemon juice
Grated zest and juice of
    1 small orange (about
    1 tablespoon grated zest
    and 1/4 cup juice)
Crème fraîche or sour cream,
    for garnish
  1 tablespoon chopped fresh
    dill, for garnish

their juices), until tender, about 7 minutes. Add the garlic, and cook for another minute or two.

Stir in all the remaining ingredients, except the garnishes. Simmer over low heat, uncovered, for at least 1 hour, or until all the vegetables are tender. Taste for the sweet and sour balance, and correct with a splash of orange or lemon juice if need be.

This rich and tangy soup can be served piping hot right out of the pot, or chilled for a hot-weather meal. If prepared a day in advance and serving chilled, check the seasoning—the refrigerator chill will dampen the flavors.

Top with a swirl of crème fraîche or sour cream and a sprinkle of chopped fresh dill.

Serve with fresh, home-baked rye bread or pumpernickel, with a crock of sweet Hoggett butter—and mugs of good, cold beer or ale.

MAKES 8 TO 10 SERVINGS

Sautéed Winter Parsnip Soup with Scallions

"Fresh garden parsnip soup in the dead of winter!" Mrs. Hoggett announces. "Oh, it's easy if you know your vegetables." And of course she does. She purposely leaves an ample supply of parsnips buried in the ground when autumn rolls around and frost spells the end of fresh vegetables. Then, whenever there is a melt or partial thaw, she scurries into the garden and digs up a handful of the white roots for a soup or a dinner dish. "They grow sweeter if you leave them underground in winter," says the sage of Hoggett Hollow.

2 tablespoons unsalted butter

6 parsnips (about 1 3/4 pounds), peeled and chopped

6 scallions, trimmed and chopped

1 1/2 quarts Savory Vegetable Stock (page 36), canned vegetable stock, or water

1/2 cup parsley sprigs, chopped

1 cup heavy cream

1 sprig fresh tarragon, chopped

1/2 teaspoon salt

Freshly ground black pepper, to taste

1/3 cup diced smoked mozzarella cheese

Snippets of parsley or chives

In a soup kettle, heat the butter over medium heat. Add the parsnips and scallions, and sauté until they are lightly browned, about 5 minutes.

Add the vegetable stock or water, and the parsley. Simmer, partially covered, until parsnips are tender, 25 minutes.

Remove the solids with a big slotted spoon to a food mill and force through over a bowl. Or, if lacking a food mill, place the solids in a food processor, add a little liquid from the pot, and puree until smooth. In either case, stir the puree back into the soup in the pot.

Stir in the cream, and gently reheat the soup. Add the tarragon, salt, and pepper to taste, and the smoked mozzarella. Remove the pot from the heat.

Ladle into bowls, and garnish with parsley or chives.

Serve with country bread and a creamy Jack cheese or Tilsit.

MAKES 6 SERVINGS

Wild Mushroom Soup

No sooner had Babe shown his talents as a sheep-pig than the Boss's mushroom light went on. "Come, Pig," he said, leading the way into the dark oak and spruce woods. The Boss's old way of hunting chanterelles was to walk through the forest, head bent, eyes on the carpet, searching for a hump or bulge in the dead leaf cover—a sign of fungi pushing up underneath. He was certain that Babe, given a "truffle-pig" hat to wear, would provide him untold new bounty. Snout to the turf, the pig did, rooting up many mushrooms. But there was a tradeoff. It was two for Babe, one for the pot. The Boss *couldn't* deny him. Babe came back belching and grinning, and the Boss ended up with about the same number of chanterelles as before. Unless you absolutely know for sure which mushrooms are safe to eat, go harvesting in your market.

2 pounds fresh chanterelles or other wild mushrooms to your liking, or even the lowly button mushroom is good in this soup
1/4 cup olive oil
1 large onion, thinly sliced
2 quarts water
1/2 teaspoon salt, or to taste
Freshly ground black pepper, to taste
1/2 cup heavy cream

Wipe mushrooms clean. Trim and slice. In a kettle, heat oil over medium heat. Add onion and sliced mushrooms, and cook, stirring, until moisture from mushrooms is cooked away and onion just begins to brown, at least 4 minutes.

Pour the 2 quarts of water into the pot, scraping the bottom to loosen any crusty pieces. Season with salt and pepper, and add cream. Simmer, partially covered, for 30 minutes.

In batches, lift solids from soup with a large slotted spoon and place in a blender or food processor, add a little liquid from pot, and puree. Pour the puree back into pot.

Ladle into 8 bowls and serve piping hot. Float little garlic or Parmesan croutons on top of the soup for added crunch.

MAKES 8 SERVINGS

The Boss's Iced Potato-and-Leek Soup

When the sheep are throwing tantrums at dipping or shearing time, and the Boss comes in hot and parched from eating their dust all morning, Esme knows the perfect noontime palliative. Hoggett sighs with satisfaction. Her iced potato-and-leek soup, he confided to the Parson one Sunday, is better than his own *mother's*, God rest her soul. It is all in the leeks, the Boss says, and Esme's have the sweetest aroma, and the tenderest natures in the region. She speaks the lost language of leeks, he believes.

2 tablespoons unsalted butter
2 cups chopped leeks (mostly white part, a little green), rinsed well
1/2 cup chopped onions
2 cups thinly sliced Yellow Finn or boiling potatoes (peeled or not, as you wish)
2 cups water
1 teaspoon salt
1/2 teaspoon freshly ground white pepper
2 cups milk
1/2 cup heavy cream or sour cream (optional)
Crème fraîche or sour cream, for garnish (optional)
Sprinkle of chopped fresh chives
Sprig of fresh parsley, chopped

In a soup kettle , heat the butter over medium-low heat. Add the leeks and onions, and cook slowly, stirring occasionally, until leeks reach a buttery texture, 6 to 8 minutes. Add the potatoes and water, and simmer, partially covered, until they are tender, 25 minutes. Season with salt and pepper.

Reserve 1 1/2 cups of the soup un-pureed. In batches, transfer solids with a slotted spoon to a food processor, add a little liquid from the pot, and puree. Stir back into the pot. Add un-pureed portion. Add the milk and cream. Simmer a bit to blend flavors, but do not boil.

Let cool and refrigerate for an hour or more. Taste for salt and pepper—chilled soup takes more seasoning.

Ladle into chilled bowls. In a small bowl, whisk the crème fraîche to loosen, and dribble on each. Add herbs.

Serve with bruschetta, topped with tomato and feta.

MAKES 6 SERVINGS

Summer Cucumber Soup with Chopped Walnuts

An invigorating surprise for a hot summer day: a soothing cucumber-yogurt balm with a spicy cayenne-garlic kick. "This requires *no* cooking," Mrs. H. says. "What do you think of that?" It's a wonderfully delicious first course that is easy and can be made well ahead of time.

2 *hothouse cucumbers*
  (they're the long ones)
1 *teaspoon salt*
2 *cups unflavored yogurt*
1/3 *cup chopped walnuts*
2 *tablespoons minced*
  fresh dill
2 *teaspoons minced garlic*
Cayenne pepper, a sprinkling
2 *tablespoons extra-virgin*
  olive oil
4 *teaspoons mango chutney*

Peel the cucumbers and slice in half lengthwise. Scoop out and discard the seeds. Dice the cucumber finely and neatly—1/4-inch cubes. Place in a small bowl and sprinkle evenly with 1/2 teaspoon of the salt. Set aside at room temperature for 15 minutes.

Wash the cucumber briefly in a sieve under cold running water. Drain, and dry thoroughly between paper towels.

Combine the cucumber, yogurt, walnuts, dill, garlic, cayenne, and the remaining 1/2 teaspoon salt in a deep bowl. Stir in the olive oil.

Refrigerate an hour or more until cold, then verify the seasoning, adding more salt or dill as needed. Ladle into chilled bowls and serve immediately. Garnish each with a teaspoon of chutney.

A tall, cool glass of water from the springhouse—that's all you need as an accompaniment.

MAKES 4 SERVINGS

A Garden of Salads

"Greens are not just for the rabbits or the Pig.

Oh my, no!"

Salads bloom in the Hoggett's sunny kitchen as though they grow there, indoors. Babe noses among the baskets and bowls of freshly picked fruits and vegetables, entranced by the colors, the bursts of fragrance. He twitches, watches—fascinated—as Mrs. H. creates her salads with an artist's palette: greens, golds, reds, oranges, purples. Babe marvels: Why not just snarf the darn stuff as is? It's fabulous! How could it be any better? Esme sometimes agrees.

A tomato zealot, she'll slip unseen, after a long deprived winter, between the rows of early summer vines, pluck two or three red ripe specimens off the stems, and just fang them, gobbling the luscious fruits, with juice and seeds running down her arms. It's true—Esme knows no shame when it comes to sweet new tomatoes. Whoever does?

She scoops up her salad harvest from one end of the garden to the other and from the orchard and the berry patches down by the stream: fresh spinach and strawberries, fennel, baby leeks, and Belgian endives. And such creations. There is an Apple-Tangerine Salad with Chèvre and a salad inspired by a psychedelic new Swiss chard; an American-style picnic potato salad and a Country French Forestière Salad. And more.

Country French Forestière Salad

It's the favorite of the Man of the House, this delicious warm salad—mushrooms and mesclun of greens, tossed in a crème fraîche-balsamic dressing with Parmesan croutons. *Forestière* in French country cooking means anything with wild forest mushrooms—porcini, cèpes, morels, or other edible exotics. But shiitake or oyster mushrooms are also fine in this dish and widely available. Mrs. H. uses a mesclun of frisée (sweet curly endive), Bibb lettuce, one or two other leaf lettuces, escarole, and baby spinach. A true Provençal mesclun is a mixture of French baby greens—arugula, chervil, chickweed, dandelion, and oak leaf lettuce—but the possibilities are infinite. "You won't believe what French farm women do to make this salad a meal," Esme says. "Dump piping hot French fries right out of the fryer into the salad, they do. Toss the fries in the dressing. Delicious! Those French—what *don't* they know about eating!"

12 cups mesclun (*mixed baby greens*)

3 cups assorted fresh mushrooms, such as shiitake, chanterelle, porcini, oyster, or any edible wild mushrooms

1 small baguette

3/4 cup extra-virgin olive oil, just about

3 tablespoons freshly grated Parmesan cheese, for the croutons

Salt and freshly ground black pepper, to taste

Rinse the greens and spin or pat them dry. Tear into small pieces. Stem the mushrooms, and clean by gently rubbing with a damp paper towel. Cut into 1/4-inch-thick slices. Reserve.

Preheat your oven to 450°. Cut the baguette into 16 thin slices. Brush each slice with a little olive oil, about 1 1/2 teaspoons, and sprinkle with Parmesan. Place them on a baking sheet, cheese side up, and toast in the oven until light golden brown, about 5 minutes. Reserve.

In a roomy skillet, heat 3 tablespoons of the olive oil over high heat. Add the sliced mushrooms with a little salt and pepper, and sauté until golden brown, about 5 minutes. Add the garlic, shallots, and herbs, and sauté 30 seconds more.

3 cloves garlic, finely chopped
2 tablespoons finely chopped shallots
2 tablespoons chopped mixed fresh herbs (choose any three: basil, chervil, chives, rosemary, tarragon, thyme)
1/2 cup crème fraîche or sour cream
1/4 cup balsamic vinegar

Turn the hot mushroom mixture into a large salad bowl. Whisk the crème fraîche or sour cream in a small bowl to loosen it up, and then fold it along with the balsamic vinegar into the mushroom mixture. Taste for seasoning, and add salt and pepper if needed.

Add the greens and toss well. Divide immediately among 4 to 6 plates. Surround with the warm toasts, and serve while the salad is still warm.

Pour a chilled glass of fumé blanc—perfect.

MAKES 4 TO 6 SERVINGS

Strawberry-Spinach Salad with Toasted Sunflower Seeds

A favorite at Country Women's Association luncheons, this attractive, many-flavored composition tickles all the different taste buds, and helps the members to keep their lovely figures. "Oh it's a pretty one, it is," Esme says. "Bright red berries, pale green kiwi against dark green spinach." She serves it as a starter course, making it with almost any kind of sweet tender berries or other fruit in season. Use small delicate spinach leaves—either the smooth or the crinkled Bloomsdale variety is good as long as it's young and not yet leathery. Spinach goes well with a robust, flavorful dressing, such as this fruit-and-wine-vinegar vinaigrette.

(continued)

8 cups small tender spinach leaves

1/3 cup hulled sunflower seeds

1 pint fresh strawberries

2 ripe kiwifruit or other seasonal ripe fruit (optional)

RASPBERRY VINAIGRETTE

1/2 cup extra-virgin olive oil, or your preferred salad oil

1/4 cup raspberry vinegar

1 tablespoon sherry wine vinegar

1 shallot, finely minced

Salt and freshly ground black pepper, to taste

Thoroughly rinse, stem, and dry the spinach, and chew a leaf to be sure you've removed all grit. Tear or cut into wide strips, and place in a large salad bowl. Reserve.

PREPARING THE SUNFLOWER SEEDS: In a cast-iron or other heavy skillet, without oil, toast the seeds over medium-high heat 4 or 5 minutes, shaking the pan frequently. Remove the seeds from the pan immediately when they are golden brown, and toss into a bowl.

PREPARING THE FRUIT: Wash, hull, and dry the strawberries. Halve or slice them neatly. Peel and thinly slice the kiwifruit, if using. Reserve.

MAKING THE DRESSING: In a small bowl, whisk together the oil, the vinegars, shallot, and salt and pepper to taste. Pour the vinaigrette over the spinach and toss well.

ASSEMBLING THE SALAD: Divide the spinach among 4 salad plates. Sprinkle the sliced strawberries on all 4 salads. Arrange the kiwifruit slices attractively, if using. Sprinkle the roasted sunflower seeds over each salad.

Serve at room temperature for the best flavor.

Make sure each guest has a handful of freshly baked bread so they aren't reduced to using their fingers to mop up the last drops of vinaigrette.

MAKES 4 SERVINGS

Avocado-Tomato-Mushroom Salad with Country Mustard Vinaigrette

"Well, what are we waiting for? Get a wiggle on," Esme Hoggett says to her wide-eyed niece, who is marriage-bound and has come, at the urgent behest of her intended, to learn a few kitchen secrets at the apron hem of the master. "Can't go wrong with this delicious chopped salad!" It's simple—a little chopping, dicing, and whisking, and the bride-to-be will have an elegant, savory dish that will delight and impress. But this *is* the niece who, on their first date, gave her future fiancé a glass of grapefruit juice that was actually sauerkraut; who served him a dinner of all pureed food; who stuck a loaf of bread in a paper bag in a 500° oven to warm it up and set the kitchen afire; who gave a dinner party for her fiancé's boss and used a head of garlic instead of just a clove in the chilled cucumber soup; and who served a spinach salad with so much grit they could hear loud crunching around the table. Not to worry. This perennially popular salad at Esme's table is almost foolproof: a delectable mix of cool tastes and contrasting textures, held together by the velvety, piquant vinaigrette.

COUNTRY MUSTARD
VINAIGRETTE
- 1 tablespoon whole-grain country mustard
- 1/2 teaspoon Dijon mustard
- 1 tablespoon sherry wine vinegar
- Salt and freshly ground black pepper, to taste
- 1/3 cup extra-virgin olive oil, or your preferred salad oil

MAKING THE VINAIGRETTE: In a good-size bowl, whisk together the two mustards, the sherry wine vinegar, and the salt and pepper. Whisking constantly, add the oil in a thread—slowly enough so it emulsifies as you go and the dressing takes on a smooth, creamy consistency. (If you add oil too fast, the vinaigrette will break and separate and you'll have to start over.) Taste for seasoning, and adjust if needed. Reserve.

(continued)

12 large button mushrooms
2 ripe avocados
2 large ripe tomatoes
8 large, pretty butter lettuce
  leaves
Snipped fresh chives (optional)

MAKING THE SALAD: Brush or wipe the mushrooms clean with a damp paper towel. Stem the mushrooms and dice the caps into pretty 1/4- to 1/2-inch pieces.

Pit and peel the avocados, and cut into 1/4- to 1/2-inch dice. Core the tomatoes, and cut into 1/4- to 1/2-inch dice.

Rinse and dry the lettuce leaves, and cut the stem from the bottom of each. Arrange 2 leaves as a bed on each of 4 chilled plates.

In a large bowl, gently toss the diced avocados, tomatoes, and mushrooms together with the vinaigrette. Heap a large mound atop the 4 lettuce beds.

Serve immediately while still chilled. Garnish with fresh chives, if you like.

A perfect first course or a satisfying lunch salad. Excellent with a glass of Merlot or Cabernet.

MAKES 4 SERVINGS, BUT CAN BE EASILY DOUBLED
OR TRIPLED

Viking Purple Potato Salad with Oniony Lemon Dressing

"Blue potatoes, gold potatoes, red potatoes—oh, it's a wonderful time to be alive, don't you think?" Mrs. Hoggett says. "Who'd've thought you could dress up the drudgey old potato and take her to the ball?" The new varieties of potatoes are indeed princesses. Rose Finn, Red Russians, Red LaSodas are all excellent in potato salads—moist, waxy-fleshed, dense rather than mealy, they absorb dressings without falling apart. Esme personally prefers the new blues for her creamy, crunchy, slightly tangy potato salad. "Viking Purples, All Blues, Purple Peruvians—they just ooze flavor," she says. "Sweet, a wee bit nutty. And you know they pick up the blue in my kitchen tiles! I know—silly me." Real new potatoes—freshly harvested summer or fall potatoes—are the sweetest and most delicate to eat no matter which variety you use. This classic dish will taste of your youth, of collapsing ravenous at the picnic table, having given your all at family-reunion softball, and digging into Mother's own potato salad.

1 1/4 pounds small purple
　　potatoes, scrubbed (leave
　　their skins on)

DRESSING
　1 cup mayonnaise
　Juice of 1/2 lemon
　1 tablespoon cider vinegar
　2 tablespoons minced
　　fresh parsley
　2 teaspoons Dijon mustard

Into a pot of 2 quarts cold, lightly salted water, drop the potatoes. Bring to a boil. Then reduce the heat and simmer for 15 to 25 minutes, or until the potatoes are fork-tender. Drain in a colander and let cool. Cut into 1/2-inch dice. Some of the skins will come off, some won't. That's fine. Place the potatoes in a large bowl.

MAKING THE DRESSING: In an ample bowl, thin the mayonnaise with the lemon juice and cider vinegar. Whisk in the parsley, mustard, celery seeds, dill, and salt and pepper to taste. (You may not need salt; prepared mayonnaise has sufficient salt already.) Stir in the scallions and radishes, if

1/2 teaspoon celery seeds
1/2 teaspoon finely minced
    fresh dill
Salt and freshly ground black
    pepper, to taste
1/2 cup chopped scallions
1/4 cup sliced radishes
    (optional)

1 1/2 cups diced celery
    6 large pretty leaves of red
      leaf or other lettuce

GARNISHES
    6 to 8 ripe plum tomatoes,
      cut into wedges
    Dill pickles or sweet pickles,
      sliced or cut into thin strips

using. Let sit for about 20 minutes to allow the oniony-tangy flavors to develop.

MAKING THE SALAD: Add the diced celery to the dressing, and then pour the dressing over the cooled potatoes. Toss together gently. Don't skimp with the amount of dressing—the potatoes will absorb a lot of it. Cover and let sit for at least an hour before serving, either at room temperature or in refrigerator.

Wash and dry the pretty lettuce leaves. Arrange as beds on 6 salad plates. Mound the potato salad in the center of each leaf. Slice the plum tomatoes in wedges, and surround the salads. Garnish with the pickles, or other garnishes of your choice.

One of Esme's kitchen maxims: Potato salad ripens with time.

MAKES 6 SERVINGS

radishes

Braised Baby Leeks with Roasted-Tomato-and-Herb Sauce

"Yes, Reverend Small spoke briefly, much to the delight of the congregation," Mrs. Hoggett reported to her daughter on the telephone. "But then the poor man took ill, so Wednesday's healing services have been canceled until further notice. Sometimes I wonder about that church. Well, no matter. He asked to have some of my braised baby leeks, which he *adored* the last time he— What *is* that smell?! Oh my gosh, oh my golly, I've incinerated the tomatoes! Can't talk!" She hung up and bustled to take the charcoaled tomatoes off the burners and started over, for the good Reverend's sake. It *is* a delicious and unforgettable salad. Delicate aromatic leeks coddled in a savory roasted-tomato-and-herb sauce—a dish to get well for fast. Prepare the sauce at least two hours ahead, if not overnight, to allow the flavors to develop fully.

12 *fresh baby leeks, or very small leeks*

2 *quarts water or canned vegetarian "chicken" broth (visit your health food store for this one)*

1/2 *teaspoon salt, if using the water*

PREPARING THE LEEKS: Trim the roots and tops from the leeks, cutting an inch or so above the Y, where the stalk joins into the root end, and saving the largest, prettiest tops for garnishes. Split the leeks lengthwise down toward the root end, but without cutting all the way through the end. Bathe the leeks under cold running water, removing mud and sand.

In a saucepan, cover the leeks with the water or broth, and season with the salt if using the water. Bring to a boil. Then reduce the heat to a simmer and braise gently, uncovered, for 20 to 40 minutes, or until the leeks are buttery tender. The cooking time will depend on how young the leeks are.

(continued)

1 tablespoon mixed fresh
  herbs, chopped (choose
  any three: basil, chives,
  rosemary, tarragon)

3 ripe plum tomatoes

2 teaspoons tomato paste

1/3 cup extra-virgin olive oil,
  or your preferred salad oil

1 tablespoon sherry wine
  vinegar

1/4 teaspoon freshly ground
  white pepper, or to taste

Fresh herb sprigs, for garnish
  (optional)

Remove the cooked leeks from the liquid and allow to cool to room temperature. (Cooked, the leeks will keep refrigerated for 2 or 3 days.)

MAKING THE SAUCE: Chop 1 tablespoon of your chosen three herbs. Reserve.

Roast the tomatoes over an open flame on the stove, or under the broiler, for just a minute or so, turning often to char the skins all over. Immediately flake the charred skins off under cold running water. Core and halve the tomatoes. Then squeeze each half in your hand, removing the seeds and juice—scoop out the seeds with a fingertip. Reserve one-third of this tomato meat. Place the other two-thirds of the tomato meat in a blender with the tomato paste. Puree 30 seconds, while adding the olive oil in a thread—the mixture should be smooth and creamy.

With the blade stopped, add the vinegar and your selection of chopped herbs. Season with salt and pepper. Mix with a short burst of the blender. Pour the liquid into a glass or ceramic bowl.

Finely chop the reserved one-third of the tomato meat and stir this into the sauce by hand, and let the whole mixture sit at least 2 hours to allow the flavors to develop and mingle.

PREPARING THE GARNISH: When ready to serve, blanch the reserved raw green leek tops in boiling water for just the count of three. Then immediately chill in an ice bath to set the vibrant green color and tenderize. Cut these naturally folded greens on the bias in 1/4-inch strips. Unfold to form chevrons or U shapes. Aren't they beautiful?

ASSEMBLING THE SALAD: Pool the tomato-herb sauce onto the center of 4 chilled salad plates. Top each with 3 leeks. Arrange the pretty green chevrons around the edge of each plate, garnish with herb sprigs if using, and serve immediately.

A hot-from-the-oven baguette or other good, fresh bread is *de rigueur* for sopping up this sauce—you may not need to wash the plates.

MAKES 4 SERVINGS

"Bright Lights" Swiss Chard with Sun-Dried Tomatoes

Opening her new seed catalogue to the "Annual All-World Selections in Bedding Plants and Vegetables," Esme caught her breath. "Out-*rageous!*" she squealed. "Oooh my! The C.W.A. Summer Competitions . . . purple with envy . . . must order now . . . Where's that pen?" What set her scurrying was the top award-winner, a new Swiss chard named "Bright Lights" for its show-stopping colors: brilliant pink, gold, violet, and orange stems with colored veins snaking up through deep green and magenta leaves. A gorgeous, crowd-pleasing salad bloomed in Esme's mind's eye—and here it is. The milder flavor of "Bright Lights"—an improvement over other Swiss chards—makes it a perfect salad candidate. (If it's not available, Ruby, Vulcan, or other red-stemmed chards make a bold salad.) Chard leaves are fairly tough, so choose the youngest plant, the tenderest leaves. Here the tangy flavor of the chard is balanced by the complex sweetness of the lemon-sherry-mustard dressing, with the diced bits of stalk adding welcome color and crunch. Mrs. Hoggett grows this chard in her flower garden as a decorative plant as well.

1/2 cup pecan halves
1 large bunch young, sweet "Bright Lights" Swiss chard
1 large bunch watercress
1 head Butterhead lettuce (Bibb or Boston)

ROASTING THE PECANS: Preheat your oven to 250°. Very carefully roast the pecans on a baking sheet in the oven for 6 to 8 minutes, or until they smell nutty and turn golden brown. They burn easily, so watch closely. Set aside to cool.

PREPARING THE GREENS: Wash the chard, watercress, and lettuce thoroughly, and spin or blot dry.

Stem the chard and tear the tenderest, sweetest leaves into small pieces. Save the prettiest pink, gold, pink, violet, and orange stems. Cut and dice the top inch or so of a few of the

1/4 pound button mushrooms
or more exotic varieties,
such as chanterelles
or shiitake

DRESSING

2 tablespoons dry sherry

2 tablespoons fresh lemon
juice

1 clove garlic, minced

1 teaspoon Dijon mustard

Salt and freshly ground
white pepper, to taste

6 tablespoons extra-virgin
olive oil, or your preferred
salad oil

2 tablespoons chopped
sun-dried tomatoes
(oil-packed)

stems—about half a cup—to give crunch to the salad. Cut the remaining pretty stems into 2-inch pieces with their ends trimmed at attractive angles, to use as garnish.

Cut the tough stems off the watercress. Tear the lettuce in large leaves.

Combine all the greens plus the diced chard stems in a large bowl, and reserve.

PREPARING THE MUSHROOMS: Remove any tough stems from the mushrooms. Wipe clean with a damp paper towel. Slice thinly. Reserve.

MAKING THE DRESSING: In a small bowl, whisk together the sherry, lemon juice, garlic, mustard, and salt and pepper to taste. Whisk in the olive oil in a thread so the dressing becomes creamy.

ASSEMBLING THE SALAD: Pour the dressing over the salad, and toss well. Lightly mound the salad on 4 plates, and turn a few of the larger chard leaves up to show their veiny color. Top each salad with a sprinkle of mushrooms, toasted pecans, and sun-dried tomatoes. Arrange the beautifully hued pieces of chard stems in a pleasing pattern around the edge of each salad.

Serve with a fresh sourdough baguette, or with warm goat cheese crostini—shreds of cheese laid on warm, small toast rounds, with a drizzle of olive oil.

MAKES 6 SERVINGS

Endive Salad with Roasted Hazelnuts

"Walnuts, yes—fine with Belgian endives," Mrs. H. says. "But roasted *hazelnuts* with endives—blissful!" Roasted hazelnuts give new meaning to the term "nuttiness." Once you take in the aroma, once you taste them hot out of the oven, you are at their mercy. They will damage your character and make you consume indiscriminately. Babe, fed a handful once by the Boss, now has to banish himself to the far pasture whenever he smells them cooking, lest he make a fool of himself by standing at the kitchen door crying. This simple, sweet-bitter-crunchy salad is one of Esme's most widely acclaimed.

COUNTRY MUSTARD
VINAIGRETTE

- 1 tablespoon whole-grain country mustard
- 1/2 teaspoon Dijon mustard
- 1 tablespoon sherry wine vinegar
- Salt and freshly ground black pepper, to taste
- 1/3 cup extra-virgin olive oil, or your preferred salad oil

- 1/2 cup hazelnuts
- 6 medium-size Belgian endives
- 2 ripe tomatoes, or about 20 red, yellow, and orange cherry tomatoes

MAKING THE VINAIGRETTE: In an ample bowl, whisk together the two mustards, the sherry wine vinegar, and the salt and pepper. Whisking constantly, add the oil in a thread—slowly enough so it emulsifies as you go and the dressing becomes glossy and smooth. Taste for seasoning. Reserve in the bowl.

TOASTING THE HAZELNUTS: Preheat your oven to 350°. Spread the hazelnuts on a baking pan and roast in the oven for 10 to 12 minutes, or until medium golden brown, shaking the sheet once or twice to roll them over for even browning. Watch carefully—they burn very easily, and then you'll have to start over again. If you don't want to turn on the oven, toast the nuts in a dry skillet over medium heat, shaking the skillet occasionally. Same warning here—watch carefully.

Let the roasted nuts cool slightly, then rub between your palms or in a clean kitchen towel to flake off the skins—some small pieces of skins may remain, but not to worry. Coarsely chop the peeled hazelnuts, and reserve.

MAKING THE SALAD: Peel off and reserve 20 large, perfect endive leaves. Slice the remaining endives diagonally into 3/4-inch sections, which will break apart into separate pieces.

Add the sliced endive spears and the chopped hazelnuts to the vinaigrette in the bowl, and toss well.

With the whole endive leaves, make a star on each of 4 salad plates. Mound a quarter of the salad at center of each star.

Core the tomatoes and slice each one into 10 wedges. Or if using the cherry tomatoes, cut them in half. Arrange 5 of the tomato wedges or 10 cherry tomato halves around each salad plate, alternating with the whole endive leaves.

Serve immediately.

A fabulous starter course that goes deliciously with a dry white wine.

MAKES 4 SERVINGS

Bitter Greens with Pear and Crumbled Stilton

"This is the bitterest of salads, this is the sweetest of salads, it has the most assertive vinaigrette, it has the most velvety of fruit, it conceals the crunchiest of nuts, it reveals the softest cheese, its fragrant nut oil lulls my nostrils, its zesty Stilton bedazzles my tongue—in short, this salad is so far unlike any other in the uncommon range of its textures and flavors that I can speak of it in the superlative degree of comparison only." Thus spake Uncle Southcott—*Professor* Southcott—on his biannual visit to Hoggett Farm, on the occasion of tasting his niece Esme's salad of bitter greens with pear. Talking was his *forte*, this tall, white-maned Emeritus Professor of Comp. Lit., and the only time he shut up was when he had Esme's food in his mouth. Thus cooked Esme, with great vigor and incessantly, during his entire stay, the better to keep the tidal flow corked. "To be fair to the silly old darling," Esme says, "it *is* an exquisite salad."

WALNUT-SHERRY WINE VINAIGRETTE:

- 2 tablespoons sherry wine vinegar
- 2 shallots, minced
- 1 small clove garlic, minced
- 1 tablespoon coarse whole-grain mustard
- 1 teaspoon Dijon mustard
- Salt and freshly ground black pepper, to taste
- 3 tablespoons walnut oil
- 3 tablespoons extra-virgin olive oil, or your preferred salad oil

MAKING THE VINAIGRETTE: In an ample bowl, whisk together the vinegar, shallots, garlic, the 2 mustards, and salt and pepper to taste. Combine the walnut oil and olive oil in a small bowl, and whisk them into the vinegar-mustard mixture in a thread, until the dressing is thick and glossy. Taste for balance and fix, if needed. Reserve.

TOASTING THE WALNUTS: Preheat your oven to 300°. Spread the walnuts on a baking sheet, and toast in the oven for about 10 minutes, or until they smell nutty and darken slightly. Quickly toss into a bowl, and reserve.

MAKING THE SALAD: Sort and trim the bitter greens. Wash and then spin or blot dry. Core and cut the pear into thin slices.

(continued)

1/2 *cup walnuts, in large pieces*

3 *quarts mixed bitter greens,*
such as frisée, escarole,
radicchio, watercress

1 *perfectly ripe pear, such as*
Red Bartlett or Comice

1/4 *cup crumbled Stilton*

Add the greens and walnuts to the dressing, and toss well. Add the pear slices, and toss gently.

Divide among 4 salad plates. Top with the crumbled Stilton.

Tuck small rounds of garlic-rubbed toast on the edges of the plates as an ideal accompaniment.

MAKES 4 SERVINGS

Marinated Fennel, Red Onion, and Chanterelle Salad

"Well, I mended the harness, sharpened tools, shaved shingles, and whitewashed the henhouse," Esme bubbled. "I repaired the garden fence, picked the peas and beans so the vines don't ripen too soon, cleaned the stalls, swept the south barn floor, blacked the stove, whetted the scythe, and set the sponge for tonight's bread. I'll make the eggnog to send out to the men in the field, then I'll be done." She sighed with great satisfaction. "Uh-oh," Babe thought, as he sat with his head cocked to one side listening to her, "she forgot one thing." Picky eater Aunt Lucy is on her way over for lunch, and she hasn't made a thing. "And for Aunt Lucy, who will love its soft anise flavor," Esme said, reaching into the refrigerator, "my marinated fennel salad! I made it a day ahead— oh, yes, it's best that way." Rich, sweet, sautéed fennel, onion, wild mushrooms—it's a fast, simple, different chilled salad. Aunt Lucy appeared at the screen door.

"Oh my," Esme said, showing her in, "do I have a tasty treat for you!"

"I probably won't like it," Aunt Lucy said, brushing past her. Esme, smiling

Cheshire cat-like, took the good woman's straw sun hat, hung it ever so carefully on the wooden peg, and swanned over to the luncheon table.

1 bulb crisp fresh fennel

1 red onion

1 1/2 pounds firm fresh chanterelle mushrooms or others such as shiitake or cremini (or white button, if those are all you have)

6 tablespoons extra-virgin olive oil, or your preferred salad oil

Juice of 1 lemon

Pinch of ground coriander

Salt and freshly ground white pepper, to taste

Trim any stalks from the fennel bulb, but save leafy green feathers for garnish. Cut the bulb into pretty 1/4-inch dice. Dice the onion similarly.

Wipe the chanterelles clean with a damp paper towel. Slice thinly—1/4-inch thick will do.

In a roomy skillet, heat 2 tablespoons of the olive oil over medium heat. Add the fennel and onion, and sauté until tender and just turning golden brown, about 4 to 6 minutes. Transfer to a large bowl.

Wipe out the skillet. Add the remaining oil, and heat over medium-high heat. Add the sliced mushrooms, and sauté until most of the moisture released from the mushrooms is cooked away, about 4 to 5 minutes. The mushrooms should still be firm. Add to the fennel mixture.

Season with the lemon juice to taste, coriander, and salt and pepper to taste. Let cool to room temperature. The salad may be served at this stage, but the best and fullest flavor will come with refrigerating the dish overnight.

Mound the salad on 4 plates, and wreathe each one with pretty fennel fronds.

A perfect lead-in to a hot soup or other warm dish.

MAKES 4 SERVINGS

Apple-Tangerine Salad with Chèvre and Tarragon-Citrus Vinaigrette

The roly-poly Mrs. H., known affectionately among the farm animals as "Her Rotundity," always has an eye to the healthy, calorie-wise dish. ("Mustn't overdo it. Must keep my figure!") This exuberant fruit salad, bursting with flavor, bursting with vitamins, satisfies her conscience and sweet tooth at the same time. The tart-sweet apple and citrus morsels make pleasing partners with the tang of the pungent fresh chèvre and peppery watercress. "Seven thousand varieties of apple out there," Esme says, "and several of the very best right on Hoggett Farm." She can choose among Pink Ladies, Winesaps, Northern Spys, or the famous Hoggett Seek-No-Furthers. You can use reliable Red Delicious, McIntosh, tart green Pippins, or Granny Smiths, or any other commercial apple. But seek out your local "antique" varieties—they may not look as sleek, but will probably be superior in taste.

1 *bunch watercress*
3 *tangerines*
2 *limes (1 of them for juice)*
1 *shallot*
1 *tablespoon tarragon vinegar*
2 *tablespoons walnut oil*
1/4 *teaspoon salt, or to taste*
1/4 *teaspoon freshly ground black pepper, or to taste*

Wash and drain the watercress. Pat gently with a clean kitchen towel or paper towels to dry thoroughly. Trim away the tough stems. Reserve.

Grate the zest of 1 tangerine and 1 lime. Juice 1 of the limes. Finely chop the shallot.

MAKING THE VINAIGRETTE: Whisk together the vinegar, lime juice, the tangerine and lime zests, and walnut oil in a small bowl until the oil is thoroughly incorporated. Add the chopped shallot. Season with the salt and pepper, and let sit for 10 or 20 minutes for the flavors to blend.

(*continued*)

1 apple
1/2 cup diced or crumbled
chèvre or French Bucheron
cheese (about
4 ounces)
1/2 cup walnut pieces

MAKING THE SALAD: Leave the peel on the apple, core it, and dice into a large bowl. Peel the remaining lime and the 3 tangerines, removing the outer white pith. Section them, remove the membranes and seeds, and add the sections to the apple along with the goat cheese and walnuts.

Pour the dressing over the fruit mixture in the bowl, and toss well.

Arrange a bed of watercress on 4 salad plates, and spoon the salad onto each bed. Serve at room temperature.

Put out a plate of buttered thin slices of toasted walnut bread or fresh French bread. This is a salad that goes especially well with an omelet.

MAKES 4 SERVINGS

The Vegetable Companions

"These are sharp-dressed vegetables—

vegetables ready to boogie."

God forbid you have a vegetable hater in the family—adult or child. But if you do, here is the perfect antidote: a handful of intriguing, delicious, different ways of dressing up vegetables for the ball. Lemon-Infused Turnips with Sweet Onion, Sweet Potatoes with Rum and Honey Tangerines, Basmati and Wild Rice with Blood Oranges—these are not disguises. These are vegetables made much of—sharp-dressed vegetables, vegetables ready to boogie. "Follow the green-and-yellow brick road," Esme tells her grandchildren, "and find these treasures!" If they still hang back—and they do, they do—she whispers the clincher: "Leprechauns are vegetarian. Oh, yes! True! Eat the sweet baby underleaves of plants, they do. Makes them so clever! Nibble, nibble." And that always tempts the children to taste the dishes. And then they're hooked.

Spinach Dumplings
with Roasted Pepper Soubise

Babe came trotting across the yard to see who this nice-smelling new human with the musical voice was. A stroke of luck that Babe did so just then, because this was the Countess Odile Paprikash, world-famous violinist and gourmet, a *soignè dame* of the first order. She was digressing from her concert tour for a special meal at the Farm, and Esme wanted to do right by her. But the hostess was in a menu tizzy. She'd planned a fine and memorable feed, of course: sumptuous soup, sparkling salad, intriguing entree, dazzling dessert—and that would do it. But no! Something was missing. What?!

The Countess, upon seeing the inquisitive Babe approach, lit up. "*Milyen gyonyoru baba!*" she cried in Hungarian. (What a beautiful baby!) She scratched the wee pig's bristly back just the way pigs *love* to be scratched. Babe shivered with pleasure. "*Ooo, quel petit dumpling! Si mignon!*"

Boing! The light went on for Esme. That's what was missing—a personalizing touch! A dish reflecting the Countess's Hungarian-French ancestry. Thus sprang from Esme's forehead this toothsome dumpling concoction with classic French *sauce soubise*: a pureed onion-butter-paprika-with-white-wine-and-roasted-pepper sauce. To die for. The whole dinner, thanks to Babe, was a great success. And afterward the Countess, having fallen hard for Babe, played him to sleep in the barn with a dreamy violin rendition of Liszt's Hungarian Rhapsody No. 20. *Gyonyoru!*

For a quick substantial soup, add these versatile dumplings to Savory Vegetable Stock (page 36) or canned vegetarian "chicken" broth.

(continued)

DUMPLINGS

> 3 *pounds fresh spinach,*
>   *cleaned, washed, with*
>   *water still clinging*
>   *to leaves*
> 1/4 *cup (1/2 stick) unsalted*
>   *butter*
> 3/4 *cup ricotta cheese*
> 2 *large eggs, lightly beaten*
> 1/2 *cup all-purpose flour*
> 1/2 *cup grated Parmesan*
>   *cheese*
> 1/2 *teaspoon salt*
> *Freshly ground black pepper,*
>   *to taste*
> *Pinch of grated nutmeg*

SOUBISE

> 1 *red bell pepper*
> 3 *tablespoons unsalted butter*
> 1 *onion, sliced*
> 1 *tablespoon paprika*
> 1/4 *cup dry white wine*
> 1/2 *cup crème fraîche*
> *Salt and freshly ground black*
>   *pepper, to taste*

MAKING THE DUMPLINGS: In a large pot, covered, steam the spinach using only the water that clings to the leaves, until wilted, 1 to 2 minutes. While this is happening, shake the pot occasionally. Remove the spinach to a colander. When cool enough to handle, squeeze out all the liquid from the spinach. Then chop it. You should have about 2 cups.

In an ample skillet, melt the butter over medium-high heat. Add the spinach and cook, stirring, for 2 minutes. Stir in the ricotta and cook, stirring, for 3 minutes more. Transfer to a bowl and let cool to room temperature.

Mix in the eggs, flour, Parmesan, salt, pepper, and nutmeg. Chill thoroughly, until the mixture is quite firm, at least 1 hour.

MAKING THE SOUBISE: Roast the bell pepper over an open flame or under a broiler, turning occasionally, until well charred on all sides, about 10 to 15 minutes. Place the pepper in a paper bag and seal. When cool enough to handle, cut the pepper in half, core, and seed. Remove the skin. From one half of the pepper, cut long thin strips for a garnish, and reserve. Coarsely chop the other half.

In a small saucepan, heat the butter over medium-low heat. Add the onion and sauté until softened, about 5 minutes. Add the coarsely chopped red bell pepper and paprika, and continue to sauté for 5 minutes. Add the white wine, and simmer for 5 minutes. Stir in the crème fraîche, and

FOR COOKING THE
DUMPLINGS

1 *tablespoon salt*

3 *tablespoons unsalted
    butter, melted*

1/2 *cup grated Parmesan
    cheese*

1 *small bunch chives,
    snipped (about
    2 tablespoons)*

simmer for 5 more minutes. Transfer to a blender and puree. (You should have about 1 1/4 cups of puree.) Add salt and pepper to taste. Pour back into a saucepan and keep warm.

Place an oven rack in the top position in your oven, and then preheat your oven to 400°.

COOKING THE DUMPLINGS: In a large saucepan, bring 1 1/2 gallons of water to a boil. Add the 1 tablespoon salt. Reduce the heat to maintain a simmer. Flour your hands well and shape the dumpling mixture into 1-inch balls. (You should have about 25 to 30.) Gently flatten each dumpling. Drop into the simmering water and cook for 5 to 8 minutes, or until the dumplings float. Remove with a slotted spoon and drain on a clean kitchen towel or paper towels.

Into a shallow 12 × 8-inch baking dish, pour 1 tablespoon of the melted butter. Arrange the dumplings in the dish. Drizzle the remaining 2 tablespoons butter over them. Sprinkle with the grated Parmesan.

Set the baking dish on top shelf of the 400° oven and bake for 5 to 8 minutes, or until the cheese melts and just begins to brown.

Remove, and spoon 5 to 6 dumplings into each of 5 or 6 bowls. Spoon the red pepper sauce around the dumplings. Garnish with the strips of red pepper and the chives.

A delicious companion dish to soup and salad.

MAKES 5 TO 6 SERVINGS

Basmati and Wild Rice with Blood Oranges

When the Chinese want to ask, How goes it? or *Ça va?* or *¿Qué tal?*, they say, "Have you eaten rice yet?" Not, mind you, "Have you managed to feed yourself today?" Certainly not "Have you eaten pizza yet?" No. It's rice that is so meaningful to them. "Eight cups of rice a day! Goodness, they are devoted to it!" Esme says. "But now, take Basmati rice—the greatest rice of all, in my humble opinion—which is grown in the Punjab, the Himalayan foothills of northern India, where they call it the 'Queen of Fragrance.' Well, Basmati rice is hardly ever eaten by the Punjabis! That's a fact! They prefer wheat bread. Go figure!" Basmati is a long-grain rice so rich and aromatic in flavor that it barely needs seasoning. With just a tablespoon or two of herbal butter and salt and pepper, it is a formidable side dish all by itself. And combined as it is here with earthy, nutty-flavored wild rice (actually a wild grass), together with the tang of citrus and crunchy toasted pecans, it is irresistible. "Oh, if I could only get those Punjabis to taste it just the once . . . "

Blood oranges are most plentiful around the first of the year, and the color of the pulp, as you can guess, is a lovely crimson.

WILD RICE

  1 *cup wild rice*
  4 *cups water*
  1/2 *teaspoon salt*

COOKING THE WILD RICE: Thoroughly rinse the wild rice in a strainer under cold running water, removing any bits of chaff. Drain. In a large heavy saucepan, bring the 4 cups of the water to a boil with the 1/2 teaspoon salt. Add the wild rice. Reduce the heat to a gentle simmer. Cover the pot and cook until the wild rice is tender but still toothy, about 45 minutes.

Pour off any remaining water. Cover and let the rice sit for another 5 minutes. Place a thin, clean dish towel inside a

1 cup white basmati rice

3 cups water

1/2 teaspoon salt

1 large blood orange, or navel orange if blood oranges are not available

1 cup pecan halves

1 cup golden raisins

4 scallions, trimmed and thinly sliced

1/4 cup extra-virgin olive oil

1/3 cup fresh lemon juice

1 bunch opal basil or other fresh basil

colander and turn the rice into it to drain. Fluff with a fork. Transfer to a large glass or ceramic bowl. Reserve.

COOKING THE WHITE BASMATI RICE: Thoroughly rinse the basmati rice in a strainer under cold running water, removing any bits of chaff. Drain. In a large heavy saucepan, bring the 3 cups of water to a boil with the 1/2 teaspoon salt. Add the basmati rice. Reduce the heat to low and simmer, covered, until rice is tender but toothy, about 10 to 12 minutes. Drain off any remaining liquid, and turn the rice into a colander lined with a thin towel to drain. Then fluff with a fork.

While the rice is cooking, grate the zest from the orange, and prepare the pecans. Toast the pecan halves on a baking sheet in a preheated 350° oven, or in a dry skillet on the stove top, until lightly darkened in color and nutty-smelling, about 8 to 10 minutes. Keep a close eye on them—nuts can burn very easily. When done, set aside.

Turn the basmati rice into the wild rice while both are still hot, and toss together. Add the golden raisins, orange zest, scallions, olive oil, and lemon juice. Toss together gently, preferably using your hands (make sure they're clean). Add salt to taste. Set aside to stand for 2 hours at room temperature to allow flavors to develop fully.

Peel the blood orange, removing the outer white pith. Cut into sections, and remove the membranes and seeds. Chill the sections.

(continued)

When ready to serve the rice, cut the basil into long thin strips.

Stir the pecans into the rice. Arrange the blood orange sections prettily on top, and garnish with the basil. Serve at room temperature.

This can be eaten as a salad by itself, or as an accompaniment with an omelet, quiche, or other egg dish.

MAKES 4 TO 6 SERVINGS

Fresh Garden Coleslaw

Many traditional coleslaws call for blanching the cabbage before adding dressing. Unblanched, though, it's crisper, fresher to the taste. Coleslaw *à la* Esme, so sweet and appealing, is a recipe her grandmother passed down to her mother—creating in Esme a slaw-aholic at an early age. She once ate so much at a picnic supper as a kid, she had a food nightmare: a giant heap of coleslaw gone mad, chasing her, overrunning her, smothering her. She got the better of it, though, without even waking up—she ate it. Never had *that* dream again. "But you know, I did see the same monster years later at a drive-in movie," she says. "Blimey!"

2 cups thinly shredded red
cabbage

2 cups thinly shredded green
cabbage

DRESSING

2 tablespoons granulated
white sugar

3/4 teaspoon dry mustard

1/4 teaspoon freshly ground
black pepper

1/4 teaspoon salt

1/4 teaspoon celery salt

Pinch of cayenne pepper

2 large eggs

1/2 cup cider vinegar

2 tablespoons unsalted butter

1/2 cup heavy cream

Place all the shredded cabbage in a large stainless steel mixing bowl.

MAKING THE DRESSING: Remove the top pan of a double boiler, and, away from the stove—before setting over boiling water—mix together the dry ingredients in the pan: the sugar, dry mustard, pepper, salt, celery salt, and cayenne.

In a small bowl, beat the eggs lightly, and add to the dry ingredients in the top of the double boiler. Then stir in the vinegar. Place the top of the double boiler over boiling water in the bottom of the double boiler. Cook the egg mixture, stirring constantly, making sure the boiling water doesn't touch the underside of the top pan. Keep stirring—you don't want those eggs to curdle.

When the dressing thickens, stir in the butter until just melted. Set aside to cool. When cold, stir in the cream. Pour the dressing over the shredded cabbage and toss well.

Cover and chill for at least 2 hours to allow the flavors to develop before serving. Taste, and adjust the seasonings, if you like.

This delectable homemade slaw is great with slices of crisp fall apples, freshly cracked walnuts, a chunk of tangy aged Cheddar. Add a glass of chilled hard cider, and you have a delightful light lunch.

MAKES 4 TO 6 SERVINGS

Friar Francisco's Devonshire Potatoes

"It's true, I did get caught by cannibals the one time," said brown-robed Brother Francis, who was passing through, raising money for his mission. That got the attention of everyone at the Hoggett dinner table, especially the grandchildren. "Oh yes I did, and I'm alive to tell about it today only because of my close attention to potatoes." Open-mouthed anticipation from his young audience.

"Why, how can that be, Father? Potatoes?" Esme asked.

"Well, you see, I noticed they had a boilin' culture. I watched them boilin' their potatoes—and then everything else they ate—in that big black pot of theirs. So when it came time for me, I said, 'Sure I'd like to oblige you fellas, but I'm a Friar.'"

Even the children groaned. Still, the pious brother's useful attention to potatoes during his travels brought home this cosmopolitan twist on his favorite English Devonshire Potatoes. A touch of gin in the mix imparts to ordinary spuds an aromatic glamour. "Essence of juniper berry," Esme says. "A match made in Heaven, it is!"

5 or 6 medium-size Yukon Gold or Yellow Finn potatoes (about 2 1/2 pounds)
2 1/4 teaspoons salt
1/3 cup buttermilk
5 tablespoons unsalted butter
1 shot of good gin
1 cup sliced fresh cremini mushrooms or white button mushrooms
1/4 cup chopped onion

Wash and peel the potatoes. Add enough water to a large pot to reach a depth of about 1 inch, and add 1 teaspoon of the salt to the water. Add the potatoes, cover the pot, and simmer until tender—about half an hour should do it. Check from time to time to make sure there is still water in the pot.

In a small saucepan, heat together the buttermilk and 3 tablespoons of the butter until the butter melts.

Preheat your oven to 350°. Butter a 9-inch glass pie dish.

Drain the potatoes, and place in an ample mixing bowl. Add the warmed buttermilk mixture and 1 teaspoon of the salt to

1 tablespoon fresh lemon
    juice
Pinch of freshly ground black
    pepper
1/2 cup crème fraîche or sour
    cream
Paprika, for garnish

the potatoes. Mash with a fork or a hand masher to achieve a rough puree. Sprinkle the shot of gin over the potatoes, and stir in well.

Place half the mashed potatoes in a thick layer over the bottom of the prepared pie dish.

In a medium-size skillet, sauté the sliced mushrooms and onions in the remaining 2 tablespoons butter until they are soft and translucent and most of the liquid is cooked away, about 4 to 5 minutes. Stir in the lemon juice, the remaining 1/4 teaspoon salt, and the pepper. Spread evenly over the potatoes in the pan, and then top with the crème fraîche. Spread the rest of the mashed potatoes over that.

Bake in the 350° oven for 30 minutes, or until lightly browned.

Remove, and sprinkle with paprika for color. Serve hot from the oven to enjoy the juniper-mushroom bouquet fully.

Some unsupervised guests have been known to eat the entire dish of potatoes on their own.

MAKES 4 TO 6 SERVINGS

Lemon-Infused Turnips with Sweet Onion

The red-headed stepchild of root vegetables! Scorned! Unwanted! In city kitchens at least. Why should that be? "Pull shining young white turnips fresh from the dirt," Esme says, "and you'll realize the battle-scarred old monsters in supermarket bins aren't turnips!" You can cut crisp young turnips into long thin strips, and serve them uncooked as finger food, with a little salt and a savory dipping sauce. "Oh, in the proper hands—I won't say whose—the turnip is as tasty as squash, as versatile as a three-blade mixer!" says the Mistress of Hoggett Farm. "It leaves the old potato in the dirt." But just boiling it won't do it. "Don't be silly. Mash it, whip it up light, add complementary flavorings—sweet onion, tangy lemon juice, and creamy crumbles of Roquefort! Yum!"

2 *pounds young turnips*
Salt for the turnip cooking
    water
1/2 *sweet onion, such as*
    Vidalia, Maui, or
    Walla Walla
1/4 *cup (1/2 stick) unsalted*
    butter, softened
1 *teaspoon sugar*
1 *teaspoon salt*
Freshly ground white pepper,
    to taste

Wash and peel the turnips, if they need peeling—if truly young, they won't. Add enough water to a large pot to reach a depth of about 1 inch, and lightly salt the water. Add the turnips, cover the pot, and simmer until tender—about half an hour should do it. Check from time to time to make sure there is still water in the pot.

Meanwhile, if you don't have a sweet onion like Vidalia, slice your "hot" onion and refrigerate in a bowl of ice water for 30 minutes or so. This will tame its harshness and sweeten it up remarkably. Drain the onion. Regardless of which onion you use, finely chop it. Reserve.

Preheat your oven to 375°.

Drain the turnips. Place them in an ample bowl, and mash them with a fork or hand masher to achieve a rough puree. Add the butter, sugar, salt, and pepper, and beat with an

3 large eggs
2/3 cup soft fresh bread crumbs
Grated zest of 1/2 lemon
2 to 3 teaspoons fresh lemon juice
1/2 cup crumbled Roquefort or Danish Blue (about 3 ounces)*

electric mixer on low speed until well mixed. Add the eggs, and beat at medium to high speed until the texture is somewhat fluffy and light.

Fold in the finely chopped onion and the bread crumbs. Stir in the lemon zest, and add 2 to 3 teaspoons lemon juice. Turn the turnip mixture into a 1 1/2-quart baking dish.

Bake in the 375° oven for 30 to 40 minutes, or until the top is lightly browned. Sprinkle the cheese over the top, and return briefly to the oven just until the cheese begins to melt. Then get it to the table. Or, you can pass the cheese separately at the table and let everyone help themselves.

*NOTE: Crumbled Stilton, Gorgonzola, or a Maytag blue cheese would be fine substitutes.

MAKES 6 TO 8 SERVINGS

Sweet Potatoes with Rum and Honey Tangerines

Garth Scrumbis is a Hoggett relative by marriage who lives so far out in the territory he has to walk toward town to hunt. Or so they say. He does not in fact hunt, as he is a pious man respectful of all God's creatures. And plenty holy in other ways—"about half preacher," according to his hired hands, who aren't allowed to swear, or spit, in his fields. Garth, wearing a pained expression, showed up at Esme's kitchen door mouthing a deferential entreaty. "My wife has, ahem, swallowed another watermelon seed, you see, and she—"

"You mean your wife is pregnant again, Garth? Come in! Come in and take that hat off!" Esme has no patience for prudishness.

"—and she has a terrible hankering for that sweet potato-and-rum concoction you are famous for," he went on. "But rum, Madam, Demon Rum in a—"

"Garth Scrumbis! You don't know pea turkey about cooking or women!" Esme could spout country with the best of the dirt kickers. "As Acting Chairwoman of the Northeast Chapter of the Country Women's Association, Third Regional Branch, I'm telling you this dish has no more alcohol once cooked than a snake has feathers! And your custard isn't cooked if you don't believe it! Now how far along is the dear girl?" Esme set about making the celebrated dish, using one of the darker-fleshed potatoes she prefers—the rich, moist new Garnet or Jewel—and prepared a treat rich enough to sweeten up even the biblically dour Garth Scrumbis.

6 medium-size sweet potatoes (about 2 pounds), scrubbed

1/4 cup (1/2 stick) unsalted butter, melted

Preheat your oven to 400°. Place the sweet potatoes on a baking sheet and bake until fork-tender, about 1 hour.

Lower the oven temperature to 375°.

When the potatoes are cool enough to handle, cut them in half lengthwise, and scrape the flesh from the skins into a

(continued)

6 tablespoons firmly packed
    brown sugar
3 tablespoons dark rum
1/2 teaspoon salt
4 Honey tangerines
2 tablespoons coarsely
    chopped pecans

bowl. Add 2 tablespoons of the melted butter, 4 tablespoons of the brown sugar, the rum, and the salt. With an electric mixer on low speed, beat until well mixed.

Grate 1 of the tangerines to remove the zest. Mix the zest into the potatoes.

Peel all the tangerines, removing the outer white pith. Cut apart the sections of 2 tangerines, and remove membranes and seeds. Fold the sections gently into the potatoes, taking care not to break them. Turn the potatoes into a 2-quart baking dish.

Section remaining 2 tangerines. Remove the membranes and seeds, and arrange the sections on top of the potatoes.

In a small bowl, stir together the remaining melted butter and sugar, and add the pecans. Sprinkle over the top of the tangerine sections on top of the potatoes.

Bake in the 375° oven for 30 minutes, or until thoroughly heated and the nuts are lightly darkened in color.

Make a meal of this with some cold whole-cranberry sauce and a spinach salad. It also makes a delicious accompaniment to the Whole-Wheat Vegetarian Pie with Shredded Asiago (page 104) or the Grilled Vegetable Sandwich with Fresh Mozzarella and Chili-Garlic Dressing (page 124).

MAKES 6 SERVINGS

Babe-Approved Suppers, Every Which Way

"Every meal is a feast—my Mum's own words, they are. She was a trifle roly-poly herself, goodness yes."

Glorious vegetables—both the summer's prizes and the winter's sleepers—find their way into heaping plates and bowls of pasta, grilled sandwiches, and even into a pie. A rich array of hot dishes, traditional and contemporary, pour out of Esme's kitchen, reflecting the bounty of all such working farms as the Hoggetts—not only fresh produce from the garden, but also bouquets of seasonings from the herb patch and mouth-watering cheeses from dairy barns near and far. It's an eclectic mix of Esme's recipes, international in origins. You'll find surprising Hosenhorne, a pastry-soufflé of German descent, which hasn't been spotted in these parts for a while, alongside a fresh vegetable pizza from heartland America; a Greek-style pasta dish with Kalamata olives, capers, and fresh Italian mushrooms; a French-style coulis (that's a fancy word for a puree) for spooning over ravioli; as well as a grilled eggplant sandwich with Indonesian flavoring. Babe lolls in his box near the stove, perpetually blissed out from the confusion of celestial smells swirling around.

Whole-Wheat Vegetarian Pie with Shredded Asiago

There is no one prouder of her kitchen garden than Esme Hoggett. "Well, now. You've got the whole darn pea patch in here, haven't you?" the Boss said the first time he forked into her vegetarian pie. He chuckled away, pleased with his wit. Esme smiled, the soul of patience. He tasted. "Hmm. Righty-oh," he murmured. Not a chuckle was heard the rest of the meal. This version includes the best of the summer harvest, but even after the freezing days and nights come to the Farm, the Boss can still have his vegetarian pie. Esme's garden moves right into her house, in a manner of speaking. Turnips, cabbages, carrots, beets, potatoes, and apples rest in their bins in the cool cellar. Squashes and pumpkins, red peppers on a thread, and onions woven into ropes share the attic with sprays of hanging dried herbs. "Oh, it's a lovely, spicy smell," the Duchess purred to Babe, "and I can go up there anytime I want."

FLAKY PIE CRUST

- 1 cup whole-wheat flour
- 1 cup all-purpose flour
- 1 teaspoon salt
- 2/3 cup solid shortening
- 5 to 7 tablespoons cold water

FILLING

- 2 tablespoons vegetable oil
- 1 small zucchini, chopped (about 1 cup)
- 3 ribs celery, chopped (about 1 cup)
- 2 medium-size carrots, shredded (about 1/2 cup)

Place a rack in the lowest position in your oven, then preheat it to 400°.

MAKING THE CRUST: In a sizable mixing bowl, stir together the two flours and the salt. Using a pastry blender or 2 knives held like a scissors, cut in the shortening until the pieces are the size of small peas. Add the water, tossing with a fork, just until the dough comes together in a bunch. Divide in half and shape one half into a disk on a lightly floured work surface. Roll out the dough into an 11-inch round, about 1/8 inch thick. Fit the circle into a 9-inch pie pan. Trim the edge, leaving a 1/2-inch overhang. Refrigerate while making the filling.

MAKING THE FILLING: In a roomy skillet, heat the oil over medium-high heat. Add the zucchini, celery, carrots,

1/2 cup sliced fresh
   mushrooms, such as
   cremini, shiitake,
   or plain button
1 small green bell pepper,
   sliced (about 1/2 cup)
1 clove garlic, minced
1 can (about 15 ounces)
   tomato sauce
1/2 cup 1/2-inch pieces of
   green beans

mushrooms, green pepper, and garlic, and sauté until just tender, about 8 minutes.

Add the tomato sauce, green beans, and all the ingredients listed under "Seasonings," except the cheese. Simmer, uncovered, for 5 minutes. Spoon into pie shell. Sprinkle the top of the filling with the Asiago—it's the smooth, creamy Asiago that weaves the dish's richness of flavors and textures into a whole. Brush the edge of the pastry with water.

(continued)

SEASONINGS

- 1 *tablespoon brown sugar*
- 1 *teaspoon dried oregano*
- 1 *teaspoon chili powder*
- 1/2 *teaspoon salt*
- 1/2 *teaspoon freshly ground black pepper*
- 1 *cup shredded young Italian Asiago cheese or Gruyère (about 4 ounces)*

THE WASH

- 1 *egg, lightly beaten*
- 1 *tablespoon water*

Roll out remaining pastry into a 1/8-inch-thick round, 10 inches in diameter, and place on the pie. Trim the overhang, and pinch edges to seal. Cut 4 or 5 steam vents.

MAKING THE WASH: In a small cup, stir together the egg with the 1 tablespoon water. Brush over the crust.

Bake the pie on lowest rack in the 400° oven for 20 minutes. Lower oven temperature to 350°, and bake 20 to 25 minutes more. Let the pie sit at least 15 minutes before cutting.

Delicious with a basket of Feather Rolls (page 32), a crock of sweet butter, and a green salad with citrus fruit and a lively vinaigrette—more vinegar than oil.

MAKES 6 TO 8 SERVINGS

Warm Linguini with Fresh Tomato, Balsamic Vinegar, and Parmigiano-Reggiano

"I tasted it and almost wept. It was moist and grainy—a shivery, salty, rich sizzle that filled my head and made my hair twitch. I could not stop eating it." That's Mary McNamara, a writer-friend of the Hoggetts, talking about cheese. *Cheese! A grown-up, level-headed woman!* Well, okay, not just cheese—the very form of cheese-ness, Parmesan variety: Parmigiano-Reggiano. She went to Italy and ate it at the source, Parma, in the Enza Valley in northern Italy, and hasn't been the same person since.

The same may be true of you once you try this elegant, room-temperature pasta. "Kitchen commandment Number One," Esme says. "Let the ingredients shine through." Sweet vine-ripened tomatoes. Fresh-from-the-garden herbs. And topping it off, ethereal Parmigiano-Reggiano. The dish has the secret of all great dishes: the purity and intensity of a few simple, strong, collaborating flavors. "It's one of my special-company offerings," Esme says. "Bless my soul—it goes together so quickly it's a sin!"

2 1/2 pounds ripe plum tomatoes

7 tablespoons extra-virgin olive oil

3 tablespoons sherry wine vinegar

2 tablespoons balsamic vinegar

1/3 cup fresh basil leaves, coarsely chopped or torn

1 tablespoon coarsely chopped or torn fresh tarragon leaves

1/2 teaspoon salt

1/4 teaspoon freshly ground black pepper

2 or 3 tablespoons minced garlic, or to taste

1 pound linguini

Curls and slivers of Parmigiano-Reggianno cheese, for finishing

Wash, core, and dice the tomatoes into bite-size pieces and place in a large glass or ceramic bowl. Stir in 6 tablespoons of the olive oil and the 2 vinegars. Add the fresh basil and tarragon. Season with the salt and pepper. Reserve.

In a small skillet, heat the remaining 1 tablespoon of the olive oil over medium heat. Add the minced garlic, and sauté until just golden, about a minute or two—don't let it brown or burn. Add to the tomato mixture, and stir. Cover the bowl with a cloth, and set aside to allow the flavors to develop for as long as you can wait, up to 5 hours.

Bring a large pot of salted water to a boil. Add the linguini, and cook until just tender, 10 to 12 minutes. Drain, turn directly into the bowl with the tomato mixture, and toss.

Divide the pasta among 6 plates, adding the tomato mixture with its liquid to each serving. Top each serving with the Parmigiano-Reggiano.

Fresh garlic bread or bruschetta is a must with this, as well as a sparkling green salad and a great red wine.

MAKES 6 SERVINGS

Risotto with Asparagus and Pine Nuts

A luscious dish in every way—flavor, texture, aroma. "A deeply tasty stock," Esme says, "the starting point for any good risotto." You *can* use oil for sautéing the onions, but here is a place where butter adds flavor to the rice. "The great secret of risotto," Esme says, "is to 'gee-up' the buggy and don't stop to feed or water till you get to the barn." Prepare the dish straight through, sit your guests down, eat. No dallying for one last tall tale. "This is rice trying to be a sauce, is what it really is," Mrs. H. says. Frequent stirring strips the starch from the rice, binds the dish, and makes it creamy. Therein lies its essential deliciousness: sauciness sparring with the toothiness of the rice.

1 1/2 quarts Savory Vegetable
   Stock (page 36) or canned
   vegetable broth
 Salt, to taste
  8 stalks fresh, slender
   asparagus
 1/2 cup pine nuts
  2 tablespoons unsalted butter
  1 onion, finely chopped
1 1/2 cups Italian arborio rice
   (look for this short-grain
   rice in the rice section of
   your supermarket)
 1/2 cup dry white wine
  2 tablespoons olive oil
  2 cloves garlic, finely chopped
 Freshly ground black pepper,
  to taste
 1/2 cup heavy cream
 1/2 cup grated Parmigiano-
   Reggiano cheese
   (see page 106), with
   more for the table

In a saucepan, bring the vegetable stock to a boil, and continue to boil to reduce it by about a cup. (If using the canned variety, don't bother reducing.) Turn the heat down, season with salt—the canned broth probably won't need any—and keep it at a low simmer.

Trim the woody stems from the asparagus, leaving just the top 6 inches or so. Slice the spears crosswise, on the bias, into thin little ovals 1/8-inch thick. Reserve.

Place the pine nuts in a large, dry skillet, and toast over medium heat, stirring frequently, until golden brown, about 5 minutes. Watch carefully, because once they begin to turn brown, they can go to unsightly black very quickly. When done, toss the nuts into a bowl so they stop browning.

In a broad, heavy pot (make sure it's not aluminum or other reactive metal on the inside, so that the wine you add later won't give the risotto an unpleasant taste), melt the butter over medium heat. Add the onion and cook, covered, until tender but not browned, 4 to 5 minutes.

Add the rice to the onion in the pot and, still cooking, stir for a minute or so to coat the grains of rice with butter.

Add the wine, and continue cooking and stirring until it is completely absorbed, a couple of minutes. Add 1 cup of the vegetable stock from the simmering pot, and cook, stirring frequently, until it is absorbed—should take 2 minutes or so.

(continued)

Add the rest of the stock in 1-cup amounts, cooking and stirring frequently until each cup is absorbed, and until you have added a total of 4 to 5 cups of stock—the rice at this point should be tender but still toothy.

COOKING THE ASPARAGUS: Between additions of stock, heat the olive oil in a large skillet over medium-high heat. Add the little asparagus ovals and the garlic, and sauté for about 1 minute, until tender. Remove the skillet from the heat and stir in the pine nuts, and season with salt and pepper. Remember to keep an eye on the risotto, adding broth and stirring.

When the last of the stock has been absorbed in the risotto (now's the time to call everybody to the table), stir in the cream and the cheese—a good big handful. The texture should be smooth and creamy. Taste for salt and cheese, and adjust if necessary.

When your guests are ready and seated at the table, top the risotto with the stir-fried asparagus and pine nuts, spoon into warm bowls, and serve immediately.

Garnish with a bit of chopped fresh thyme or Italian parsley as a variation. And make sure to have extra grated Parmigiano cheese in a bowl on the table.

MAKES 4 ROBUST SERVINGS

Hosenhorne (Rabbit Ears)

"Not real rabbit ears, mercy no—pastry," Esme says. "A soufflé with bunny ears. Oh, it's an unusual dish, it is. Have you seen it in any other cookbook?" Probably not. An endangered species even in farm country, Hosenhorne was once a highly prized main dish for Catholic farm families of German origin, especially on Friday nights back when they couldn't eat *the unmentionable.* "Arthur's brother and sisters feel they are dying and going to heaven when I make it for them," Esme says. She didn't come by the recipe easily. "I had to stand beside their mother while she cooked," she says. "A handful of this and a pinch of that—I made her put it in a container and then I measured. I don't make it very often. Oh no. Not because I don't want them to get a glimpse of heaven, but it is a bit of work. De-*licious*, though! Blimey!" The pastry tastes between a pie crust and a biscuit.

PASTRY

3 1/4 *cups all-purpose flour*
  1 *teaspoon baking powder*
  1 *teaspoon salt*
1/4 *cup (1/2 stick) unsalted butter, cut into small pieces and chilled*
1/2 *cup cold water*
1/2 *cup milk*

MAKING THE PASTRY: Preheat your oven to 400°, and grease a 13 × 9 × 2-inch baking pan. Into a large bowl, sift together the flour, baking powder, and salt. Add the butter. With a pastry blender or 2 knives held like a scissors, cut in the butter until the flour mixture looks like coarse meal. In a small bowl, mix the water and milk. Slowly dribble the liquid in, tossing with a fork until it masses together.

On a lightly floured bread board or pastry slab, gather the dough together in a thick square. With a rolling pin, roll out the dough into a 12 × 12-inch square, about 1/4-inch thick. Cut into sixty-four 1 1/2-inch squares.

Cut 1/2-inch diagonal slit in the middle of each square. Fold two corners (not the ones the ends of the slit are pointing to)

(continued)

CUSTARD

  5 *large eggs*

2 2/3 *cups milk*

  1 *teaspoon salt*

POTATO GRAVY

  1 *large potato*

  3 *cups water*

1 1/4 *teaspoons salt*

3/4 *cup all-purpose flour*

  5 *tablespoons solid vegetable
     shortening*

  1 *cup water*

under the square and pull them up through the slit, creating little rabbit ears. Place the rabbit ears snugly side-by-side in the prepared baking pan.

Bake in the 400° oven until just golden brown, about 25 minutes.

MAKING THE CUSTARD: In an ample bowl, beat the eggs well. Add the milk and salt, and mix well. Pour the mixture evenly around the rabbit ears in the baking pan.

Put the pan in the 400° oven to bake until the custard is set and a knife inserted comes out clean, about 18 to 20 minutes.

WHILE THE RABBIT EARS ARE BAKING, MAKE THE POTATO GRAVY: Peel and cut the raw potato into small cubes. Place in a medium-size saucepan with 2 1/2 cups of the water and 1/4 teaspoon of the salt. Boil until very soft but not disintegrated, about 8 to 10 minutes—don't drain.

In a large skillet, blend the flour and shortening, and stir together over medium heat until the mixture browns but doesn't burn, about 10 minutes—it should be the color of peanut butter. Add the potato with its cooking liquid, and thin it with a bit more water, to taste—as much as you need of the remaining 1/2 cup water. Salt to taste, about 1 teaspoon. Simmer the gravy, stirring occasionally, about 10 minutes. This makes a lot—refrigerate any leftovers.

TO SERVE: Cut into 48 rectangles, remove from the pan with a sharp-edged spatula, and serve about 5 per plate. Dress with the gravy.

True Hosenhorne aficionados sometimes dribble honey, maple syrup, or vinegar over the gravy. Serve with one of Esme's light soups or lively green salads or a fresh fruit salad.

MAKES 10 PORTIONS

Angel Hair Pasta in Roasted Bell Pepper Sauce with Goat Cheese

Esme and Arthur Hoggett were debating which is the better way of ripening late tomatoes: bury them in hay on the barn floor, or hang them upside down on their vines from the rafters—the advantages, the drawbacks, all the ins and outs. "Food!" howled their Daughter—she was there on a visit from the city. "Planting it! Weeding it! Picking it! When to pull parsnips! The proper way of hulling beans! How to fry apples! What goes with turnip greens?! Will too many vegetables give you the scours?! It's all we ever talk about! I can't go through another endless family dinner all about food. I'm going into town to see a movie." She stalked toward the door.

"Oh," Esme said, busy grilling a red bell pepper over an open flame. "Fine, dear. You have a nice time."

Daughter paused, sniffing. "What's that?"

"Hmm, for a sauce—roasted bell pepper, porcini, crème fraîche—"

"That sounds new."

"—with broccoli flowerets and crumbled goat cheese."

(continued)

113

"That sounds *good*. Where'd you get that recipe?"

"Oh, Mrs. Caymus up in Rutherford," said Esme, the spider to the fly.

"Really? On, like, maybe angel hair pasta?" The Daughter drifted back from the door, peering over her Mother's shoulder. "What time are we eating?"

2 cups broccoli flowerets

2 large red bell peppers

3 ripe tomatoes

2 large porcini mushrooms or your favorite mushrooms

1/3 cup olive oil

4 cloves garlic, minced

1/2 teaspoon salt

1/4 teaspoon freshly ground white pepper

2/3 cup crème fraîche

8 ounces homemade or dried angel hair pasta (capellini)

1/4 cup crumbled fresh goat cheese (about 2 ounces)

1 bunch fresh sweet basil, cut into long thin strips

In a saucepan with an inch of water, steam the broccoli flowerets, covered, until tender, about 5 minutes. Drain.

Roast the red bell peppers over an open flame or in a broiler 4 to 6 inches from the heat, turning often, until the skin is charred on all sides, about 15 minutes. Place in a brown paper bag and close. When the peppers are cool enough to handle, scrape off the skin. Remove stems, cores, and seeds. Puree peppers in a blender or food processor, and reserve.

PEELING TOMATOES: Bring a saucepan of water to a boil. Immerse the tomatoes in the water for 30 seconds to loosen the skins. Remove from the water quickly—you don't want to cook the tomatoes. Peel and seed the tomatoes, and chop.

Wipe porcini clean with a damp paper towel. Trim off any tough stems. Cut mushrooms into 1/4- to 1/2-inch dice.

In a roomy skillet, heat the olive oil over medium-high heat. Add the mushrooms, and sauté until light golden brown, 2 to 3 minutes. Mix in the tomatoes, garlic, salt, pepper, and the broccoli flowerets, and cook over medium heat to heat through, about 2 minutes. Remove from the heat, and cover.

In an ample bowl, whisk together the crème fraîche and red bell pepper puree. Thin with 1/4 cup of water or so, enough so the consistency is noticeably thinner than you think the finished sauce should be, for two reasons: Angel hair pasta is easily overwhelmed by a thick sauce; and the starch from freshly cooked pasta will thicken the sauce.

Cook the angel hair briefly in a large pot of generously salted boiling water until al dente, 2 to 3 minutes for fresh pasta, or a bit longer for dried.

Meanwhile, place the broccoli mixture over medium-low heat, tossing occasionally.

Then when the pasta is done, quickly drain well and toss immediately in the bowl with the red pepper sauce. Divide among 4 warm plates, and top each with a generous spoonful of the broccoli mixture. Top with the crumbled goat cheese. Garnish with the basil, and serve at once.

This goes well with a bitter green salad and slices of warm, fresh Italian bread for squeegeeing the luscious sauce.

MAKES 4 SERVINGS

Quiche with Broccoli, Chèvre, and Roasted Pepper

"She gets eggs in the winter when the rest of us are getting snowballs," sniffed Rose, Esme's slightly jealous neighbor, paying her the highest farmkeeper's compliment. "I do know how to talk to my chickens," Esme said, moving along the rows, talking to them in their language. "Cluck-cluck, bok-bok-bok! Very important, eggs, in a farm economy. Five cents a dozen when I was a girl. So cheap. And potatoes! Potatoes three meals a day. Had to be thrifty. Bok-bok-bok!"

2 red bell peppers
1 unbaked 9-inch pie shell
1 large egg white, lightly
   beaten
4 large eggs
2 teaspoons all-purpose flour
1/4 teaspoon baking powder
1/2 cup milk
1/4 teaspoon ground nutmeg
1/4 teaspoon salt
Freshly ground black pepper,
   to taste
1 cup coarsely chopped fresh
   broccoli (about 1/4-inch
   pieces)
1/4 cup shredded smoked
   Cheddar cheese, or other
   semi-hard cheese to your
   liking (about 2 ounces)

Roast the peppers over an open gas flame, holding with a pair of tongs, or broil in the oven 4 to 6 inches from the heat, turning as needed until blackened and blistered all over, about 15 minutes. Place in a paper bag and close. When cool enough to handle—don't want to scorch any fingers—peel off the charred skin. Core, seed, and dice the roasted pepper "meat" into small, pretty cubes. Reserve.

Preheat your oven to 425°. Line pie shell with foil and fill with dried beans or rice. Bake until just set, 10 to 15 minutes. Remove from oven and carefully remove foil with beans (save beans or rice in a coffee can for other crusts). Brush crust with egg white, and return to oven for 2 minutes. Set aside. Now the crust is sealed and won't get soggy.

Turn the oven down to 350°.

In a bowl, beat eggs. Beat in the flour, baking powder, milk, nutmeg, salt, and pepper. Fold in broccoli, half the red pepper, the Cheddar, and the chèvre. Pour into pie shell. Dot surface with butter, and sprinkle with remaining red pepper.

1/4 *cup chèvre cheese, cubed*
  (about 2 ounces)
1 *tablespoon unsalted butter*

Bake in 350° oven 45 to 50 minutes, or until quiche is set and slightly firm in center. Loosely cover crust with foil if it browns too quickly. Slide a knife into the center—it should come out clean, or practically clean.

Serve hot from the oven with a fresh fruit salad.

MAKES 6 TO 8 SERVINGS

Ravioli with Tomato Coulis and Tarragon

"A ravishing sauce, sure it is that!" Esme bubbles. "Fresh tasting. Aromatic. I don't mean to brag, but it's the only way to eat ravioli. And simple as can be. No stock, no cream, just a pure-flavored puree." Try different ravioli with it—homemade or any of the many varieties of scrumptious bite-size vegetarian ravioli available in gourmet and natural food stores. Tuscan white-bean tofu ravioli with sun-dried tomatoes and garlic is a must. Try also artichoke-and-cilantro ravioli, zucchini-onion-garlic ravioli, wild mushroom ravioli, goat cheese-and-arugula ravioli. All of them will go well with this exquisitely pure-tasting, oniony tomato coulis. "When there's a wolf in your belly," Esme says, "this will soothe it, yes it will."

8 *ripe plum tomatoes*
1/2 *onion*
3 *cloves garlic, peeled*
1 *tablespoon olive oil*
1 *shallot, minced*
1/4 *cup dry white wine or Vermouth*
2 *or 3 dozen ravioli of choice, fresh or frozen*
1/2 *teaspoon salt*
2 *tablespoons unsalted butter, softened, for extra richness if you like*
1 *tablespoon chopped fresh tarragon*
Grated Parmesan cheese, for garnish

Put a large pot of water to a boil. Salt generously.

Core and halve the tomatoes, and place them with the onion and peeled garlic cloves in a food processor. Process thoroughly, about 1 minute.

Strain the mixture through a fine strainer into a bowl, pushing through as much of the pulp as you can, using the rounded bottom of a ladle wielded in a circular motion. Alternately, if you prefer a sauce with more body and texture, don't strain out the pulp; use it as is. It's excellent either way.

In a good-size skillet, heat the olive oil over medium heat. Add the minced shallot, and sauté briefly until soft, a minute or so. Add the white wine or Vermouth, and cook until just a little bit of liquid is left, about 2 minutes. Add the tomato-onion puree, and reduce over medium-high heat until the sauce begins to thicken and is a nice sauce consistency, 15 to 20 minutes. This is the coulis.

Meanwhile, put the ravioli in the boiling water to cook.

Once the coulis is reduced to the thickness you prefer, take it off the heat and add the salt. Finish it by swirling in the softened butter, bit by bit. Adding the butter is optional, but it smoothes the sauce and blends the flavors nicely.

When the ravioli are done, drain well and place 6 to 8 on each plate, and spoon on the coulis. Sprinkle each serving with fresh tarragon leaves, chopped, or whole if they're tiny.

Serve with a dish of grated or shaved Parmesan, and a warm, fresh loaf of Italian or sourdough bread and a glass of superb wine—a Chianti would be nice. A green salad would sit on the table well—any with a robust or citrus vinaigrette is a good match.

MAKES 4 VERY GENEROUS SERVINGS

Crisp Pizza with Fontina, Gorgonzola, and Sage

The emphasis here is on fast—a quickly made but magnificently tasty light meal. This versatile olive-pepper-tomato-garlic sauce is also ideal for fettuccini, an omelet, or in other dishes that cry out for a distinctive, delicious red sauce. "And, oh my, the *cheeses*—they will make you weep. What do you think about that?" Esme says. Luxurious Italian Fontina with its fruity, nutty overtones melted in the sauce. Sharply robust Italian Gorgonzola exciting an entirely different part of the palate. "A quick trip to Paradise," Esme says. "It's a cook's dream."

10 *ripe tomatoes (about 3 1/4 pounds)*
1/4 *onion*
1/2 *red bell pepper*
8 *black olives, pitted*
5 *cloves garlic*
6 *tablespoons olive oil*
3/4 *cup (about 4 ounces) diced Italian Fontina, or Danish is good too*
1 *tablespoon chopped fresh sage*
1/2 *teaspoon salt, or to taste*
1/4 *teaspoon freshly ground black pepper, or to taste*

Preheat your oven to 325°.

Core 8 of the tomatoes, cut them into pieces, and puree them in a blender or food processor. Force the puree through a strainer into a bowl, and reserve. Peel (page 114), seed, and dice the last 2 tomatoes. Or, if you really need to get dinner on the table in a hurry, just dice the 2 tomatoes—skip the peeling and seeding. Reserve this separately from the puree.

Finely dice the onion and red bell pepper. Finely chop the olives and garlic.

In a roomy skillet, heat 5 tablespoons of the olive oil over medium heat. Add the onion and bell pepper, and sauté for a couple of minutes. Just as they begin to brown, add the pureed tomatoes, chopped olives, and garlic. Simmer over medium-high heat until the sauce begins to thicken, about 15 minutes.

1 *fresh large ready-to-use pizza bread-crust (about 12 inches), or your favorite pizza dough*

1/2 *cup (about 2 ounces) crumbled Italian Gorgonzola, or Wisconsin-made Bel Gioso—an excellent second choice*

12 *fresh basil leaves, torn into small pieces*

Add the 2 diced tomatoes. Simmer briefly. Remove from the heat, and stir in the diced Fontina and fresh sage. Season with the salt and pepper.

Brush the pizza crust with the remaining 1 tablespoon olive oil to prevent it from becoming soggy. Depending on how crisp you like your crust, pre-bake it in the 325° oven for 5 minutes. Spread the crust with about half of the sauce. You'll have some sauce left over—refrigerate to use as a pasta sauce, or for making another pizza. Sprinkle the pizza with the crumbled Gorgonzola and the torn basil.

Bake in the 325° oven for 5 minutes, or until the cheese is all melty and the sauce is hot. Cut and serve right out of the oven.

Goes nicely with a fresh fennel or mushroom salad, and with a good red wine or your favorite beer.

MAKES 6 TO 8 SERVINGS, DEPENDING ON THE SIZE OF THE WEDGES YOU CUT, WITH ENOUGH RED SAUCE LEFTOVER FOR ANOTHER PIZZA OR PASTA OR . . .

Conchiglie with Greek Olives, Capers, and Cremini

The potbellied Police Inspector had never lived a day on a farm, but he was a fount of country wisdom. "A woman and a melon are hard to know," he said, poking a honeydew with his toe. "French expression, ayup."

"Tickle it with a hoe and it will laugh into a harvest—British," Arthur Hoggett said, deadpan, humoring him. With rustlers an unceasing threat, it behooves a sheep farmer to cultivate the Law.

"Call me not olive till you see me gathered. Italian," the Inspector said.

Arthur thought a minute. "In China they say, 'Don't make a garden of your belly.'"

The portly Inspector let out a big basso laugh. "You're a funny, funny man, Hoggett. Ayup . . . Say, what's that incredible smell?"

As Arthur led the way inside, the Officer ruminated, "'Make a garden of your belly.' What exactly d' you mean by that, Hoggett?" But once he took in the full fragrance of the pasta sauce bubbling up from Esme's sauté pan—rich, woodsy perfume of morels and cremini, heavenly scent of garlic, pungent trace of capers and olives—he forgot his question entirely. Nor did he produce another aphorism until two full portions later.

"To eat well is to get your just desserts," he said. "Ho ho ho. You know, that suggests something . . ."

12 to 16 fresh cremini (about 8 ounces) or white button mushrooms

1/4 cup dried morels or porcini (about 1 to 2 ounces), or other dried mushrooms, rinsed

1 1/4 cups very hot water

With damp paper towels, wipe cremini or white button mushrooms clean. Trim tough stems, and dice mushrooms. (You should have about 2 cups of diced mushrooms.) Place the dried morels in the 1 1/4 cups very hot water in a small bowl, and let soak for 5 to 10 minutes, until softened.

Peel (page 114), core, seed, and dice the tomatoes. (You should have about 2 to 3 cups.) If you're in a hurry, you can omit the peeling and seeding.

4 large ripe tomatoes
(about 1 1/2 pounds)

6 cloves garlic, chopped

12 large Kalamata olives

12 fresh basil leaves

1 tablespoon cracked black
pepper

1/4 cup drained capers

1/4 teaspoon salt, or to taste
(optional)

1/2 pound dried conchiglie or
another favorite shell pasta

2/3 cup extra-virgin olive oil
or regular olive oil

Mince the garlic. Pit the olives, and cut them into slivers. Chop the basil.

In an ample bowl, combine the cremini, tomatoes, garlic, olives, basil, black pepper, and capers. Verify the seasoning. The olives and capers should add enough salt to the dish—if not, add a little extra salt.

Remove morels from the soaking dish, but save the flavorful water for the sauce. Strain the soaking liquid through a damp paper towel (or paper coffee filter) into a bowl. Finely dice the softened morels, and add to the tomato mixture.

Put a large pot of water on to boil. Generously salt the water. When the water is boiling, add the shell pasta.

In an extra-large skillet or wide pot or Dutch oven, heat the olive oil—the vessel has to be large enough to hold the sauce plus all of the pasta. When the pasta is about 2 minutes from being done, add the mushroom-olive-caper-tomato mixture to the skillet and briefly cook over medium-high heat, about 1 1/2 minutes. Stir in the strained morel-soaking water.

Drain pasta in a large colander. Then turn it into the skillet, and toss the sauce and pasta together. The cup-shaped shells will capture all the chunky ingredients of the sauce.

Divide the pasta among 4 plates, and serve immediately.

For soaking up the sauce, serve warm, thick wedges of a coarsely textured peasant bread.

MAKES 4 SERVINGS

Grilled Vegetable Sandwich with Fresh Mozzarella and Chili-Garlic Dressing

Honest John Larkin, the itinerant tool sharpener, was visiting the Farm on his bi-annual circuit. The amiable, talkative traveling man, who was well known for his "prodigies," sat down at Esme's table with gusto. "I come from a great line of eaters, I'll tell you," he said. "Heck, my grandmother ate spaghetti through her nose. And my great-grandfather, who invented taffy, once dug up an onion the size of his head and ate it right there in the field. Washed it down with radiator water from the tractor." Traveler John looked askance at his dinner plate: a sandwich only. But he attacked the crunchy, multi-grain, grilled-onion-and-eggplant construction with avidity, and was delighted to pronounce it remarkably hearty and satisfying. Liked the subtly smoky Mediterranean flavors of the charred vegetables. *Loved* the spicy chili-garlic dressing marrying it all. "It reminds me of the time I lunched with the Dalai Lama," he said. "He asked me to sharpen his chopsticks so he could eat his rice one kernel at a time. Why, it takes the man an entire day to finish lunch. Not a word of a lie! . . . Say, what's the secret of this *insidious* dressing?" It's *Sambal Olek*, Esme reveals, a delicious Indonesian chili-garlic paste she finds in gourmet shops and specialty food stores.

DRESSING

- 1 *cup mayonnaise*
- 1 *tablespoon* Sambal Olek, *an Indonesian chili-garlic paste, or Vietnamese chili sauce, or other Southeast Asian hot chili sauce*

Preheat your grill or, in inclement weather, your broiler.

MAKING THE DRESSING: In a small bowl, whisk together the mayonnaise and the *Sambal Olek*. Reserve.

Thinly slice on the diagonal, about 1/4 inch thick, the eggplant, tomato, red onion, and zucchini. Brush the vegetables with the olive oil, and lightly sprinkle with salt and pepper. Cut the mozzarella into 6 thin slices.

(continued)

Grilled Vegetable Sandwich with Fresh Mozzarella and Chili-Garlic Dressing and Viking Purple Potato Salad with Oniony Lemon Dressing

1   Japanese eggplant
    *(this is the small, thin
    variety, almost an
    iridescent lavender)*
1   *large ripe tomato or
    2 medium-size*
1   *small red onion*
1   *zucchini*
2   *tablespoons olive oil,
    for brushing*
Salt and freshly ground black
    pepper, to taste
2   *to 4 ounces water-packed
    mozzarella*
4   *slices multi-grain bread*

Grill the vegetables on a hot grill, or broil, for about 2 to
3 minutes each side, or until tender.

While grilling the vegetables, toast or grill the bread slices.

Spread as much of the chili-garlic dressing as you like
on all 4 slices of toast. Layer the vegetables on 2 of the
slices. Arrange 3 slices of mozzarella over the vegetables
on each sandwich.

Place the sandwich halves with the vegetables and cheese
back on the grill (cover the grill), or under the broiler, until
the cheese melts slightly, about 30 seconds. Place the top
slice of toast on the sandwiches, cut with a serrated knife
diagonally from corner to corner, and serve immediately.

A natural follow-up to one of Esme's exceptional soups.
Serve with her classic potato salad and fresh iced tea.

MAKES 2 SANDWICHES

Esme Pickles with Relish

"Don't be thinking you can just go out and buy these off the shelf! Oh, no!"

Putting up pickles and preserves may be a lost art in the hyper world of Urbia, but here at Hoggett Farm it's high art. Every smidgen of overflow from the orchard and vegetable garden, far from going to waste, goes into canning jars and pickling crocks. Babe watches mystified as cukes, onions, zucchini, eggplant, peppers, nectarines, and pears disappear under wax and rubber seal, into the larder. He squeals his porcine preference—"Eat now!"—in vain. Then through all the dour days of winter, his little eyes grow big with awe as relishes, chutneys, jellies, pickled beets and onions, candied peaches, and nectarines tumble out of the larder. "Wonders are many," Babe marvels, "but none is more wonderful than the Mrs.!"

"This is so much better than the store-bought variety," Esme says. "Oh yes. Try making your own chutney or wild blueberry jam. *So-o-o* different. Mercy, yes."

Esme's Hot and Sweet Corn Relish

They did not get along. Esme was well aware, but it was her turn to host the relatives at the end-of-summer get-together. They were all there: the dairy farmer, the citrus grower, the cheese maker, the apple grower, the wheat and oat farmer, the John Deere tractor rep, the sheep-farming Hoggetts, of course, and all their families. "Can't cook a lick," one plain-looking wife hissed about a scrawny cousin. "Feeds her hens hot water to get boiled eggs!" The cousin was busy trashing a least-favorite niece: "Pah! She gives a new name to the same stew seven days a week." The niece, a high-church type, was busting her cigar-chewing lackadaisical brother: "Yeah? well *you're* going to end up in a place where you can light that thing with your finger!" Your basic family nightmare. Esme yelled, "H*ooo-eeee!* Dinner!" and kept her fingers crossed. They all sat down to find in front of each plate a jar of Esme's homemade corn relish with a little gift card tied with a bow. On every card it said, "For my favorite relative." They all laughed. They all loved the dinner. "We had a lively time, we did," Esme says, "and got along fearfully well, considering." It was a gamble on her part, she admits, but, hey, she liked the symbolism: Her sweet-sour-spicy-peppery corn relish is a clash of flavors and textures all coming together to form one fine "pickle." Good karma for Relative Stew.

2 teaspoons finely chopped dried hot chipotle pepper (this is a dried, smoked jalapeño pepper)	In a small bowl, soak the chipotle in enough hot water to cover. Let sit softened, about 15 minutes. Drain.
12 ears fresh sweet corn	With a small, sharp knife, cut the corn kernels cleanly from the cob, without scraping the ears (you should have about 8 cups of kernels).
1/2 cup finely chopped green bell pepper	
1/2 cup finely chopped red bell pepper	In a large heavy nonmetallic Dutch oven or saucepan, combine the corn, sweet and hot peppers, onion, celery, and cabbage. Stir in the dry mustard, brown sugar, and vinegar. Add up to 1 tablespoon salt and several liberal grinds of black pepper.
1/2 cup finely chopped yellow bell pepper	
2 cups finely chopped red onion	
1 cup finely chopped celery	Bring to a boil, and then reduce the heat, cooking slowly, partially covered, for 1 hour, stirring occasionally, until the vegetables are tender but still slightly crispy.
1 cup finely chopped cabbage	
1 1/2 tablespoons dry mustard	Wash 10 half-pint canning jars with hot soapy water, rinse well, and reserve in a pot of hot water. Prepare the canning lids according to manufacturer's directions.
1 cup firmly packed light-brown sugar	
2 cups cider vinegar	

(continued)

1 tablespoon salt
Freshly ground black pepper,
   to taste
10 half-pint canning jars

One by one, remove the jars from the pot. Pour the hot relish into the jars, filling to within 1/2 inch of the top. Wipe the rims clean, put on the tops, and screw on the bands.

Transfer the jars to the refrigerator to cool. Keep refrigerated and use within 5 days.

Corn relish shines as a flavor brightener when served with mild-tasting stews, grills, and soups. Use it as a dressing in sandwiches—and as a gift for special occasions!

MAKES 10 HALF-PINTS, FOR 10 DEAR FRIENDS

A Bride's Deviled Eggs

A picnic lunch, a light supper on a sultry summer evening. "Oh yes, Deviled Eggs are a must!" Esme says, "and easy as the days are long." What cook doesn't know how to make deviled eggs? Yet the mistress of Hoggett Farm raised eyebrows the first time she made them for show. "I'll never forget," she says. "Here I'm a new bride, and Arthur's aunt was having her silver anniversary, and they asked me to help prepare the lunch, the cousins did—oh, and hefty women they were! So there's me . . . my platter of eggs . . . they were shocked! That I knew how to cook, little 110-pound *moi*! Skinny women can't cook! Very vocal about my size, they were. But oh my, I have caught up, yes I have!" The cousins made deviled eggs by dribbling a sauce of mayonnaise and spices over the hard-cooked eggs. Esme makes hers in the classic mash-and-refill style. "Creamy and spicy," she says. "Two bites of heaven!"

6 large eggs
1/3 cup mayonnaise
1 teaspoon Dijon mustard
1 teaspoon finely chopped
   scallion
1/8 teaspoon salt
1/8 teaspoon pepper
Paprika or minced parsley,
   for garnish

In a nonreactive saucepan, cover the eggs with cold water. Bring to a full boil, remove from the stove, and let the eggs stand, covered, in the hot water for 22 minutes. Transfer the eggs to a bowl of cold water, and let sit until cool.

Remove the eggs from the water. Peel them, making sure you remove every bit of shell. Cut in half the long way. Remove the yolks to a bowl, reserving the whites, and mash yolks with a fork. Add the mayonnaise, mustard, scallion, salt, and pepper, and mix with the fork until creamy.

Refill the hollows of the egg whites with the yolk mixture, using a teaspoon, or a pastry tube if the occasion requires an elegant look. Sprinkle with paprika or parsley.

There will be no leftovers.

The different things you can do to embellish and prettify stuffed eggs are almost endless. Try a pinch of curry, a healthy sprinkling of cayenne, a tablespoon of chopped black or green olives. For garnish: a selection of fresh herbs or watercress, a savory caper, or a little sliver of pickle or red or green bell pepper.

MAKES 12 DEVILED HALVES

Esme's Fabulous Dills

When Babe overdoes it on sumptuous Esme Hoggett food—and let's be frank, it happens; the wee fellow does not lean to *cuisine minceur*—he tiptoes around to the back of her herb garden and nibbles a bit of the feathery green border: Mrs. H.'s dill. He totters into the barn to sleep it off—for it's a fine natural palliative and soporific, dill is. "Oh, a pig knows these things," Esme says—even as Scandinavian mothers know to lace their children's milk with dill to soothe and lull; just as 18th-century Quakers chewed the dried root and seeds to squelch appetite during long prayer sessions. It is a delightful seasoning in modern cooking and preserving. Each of Esme's dills that follows is a bird of a different feather, but a songbird all the same.

Dilled Sweet Onion Slices

"These are a picnic and buffet-table gem," Esme says. "Ideal to tuck into sandwiches."

1 quart-size canning jar

1 to 2 sweet onions (about 1 pound), such as Vidalia or Mauii, thinly sliced

1/2 cup granulated white sugar

2 teaspoons salt

1/2 teaspoon chopped fresh dill

1/3 cup water

1/3 cup distilled white vinegar

Wash the quart canning jar with hot soapy water, rinse well, and reserve in a pot of hot water. Prepare the canning lid according to the manufacturer's directions. Remove the jar from the water. Loosely pack the onions in the jar.

In a nonmetallic saucepan, mix the sugar, salt, dill, water, and vinegar. Heat to boiling. Pour over the onions in the jar. Wipe rim clean, put the top on, and screw on band.

Transfer the jar to the refrigerator to cool. Refrigerate at least 4 hours or overnight. Use within 5 days.

MAKES 1 QUART

Dilled Garlic Cucumbers in Clabber

A bitey condiment with a traditional twist. Clabber is old New England thick sour milk or cream—that is, *real* sour cream: ripened. Crème fraîche, approximately, in today's world. The garlic and dill together are a natural.

1 cup Clabber: 1/2 cup heavy cream, chilled, plus 1/2 cup sour cream, chilled (or use 1 cup crème fraîche)

1 clove garlic

3 or 4 medium-size cucumbers

1 large red onion

2 tablespoons mild vinegar, such as white-wine vinegar

1 teaspoon salt

1 scant teaspoon granulated white sugar

1/2 teaspoon dry mustard

1/8 teaspoon freshly ground black pepper

2 tablespoons chopped fresh dill

MAKING THE CLABBER: (If using crème fraîche, skip this part.) In a bowl, stir together the heavy cream and sour cream until lightly thickened. Set aside at room temperature for 2 or 3 hours to sour a bit more.

MAKING THE CUCUMBERS: Rub a wooden salad bowl with the clove of garlic. Thinly slice the cucumbers (you should have about 8 cups of slices), the red onion, and what remains of the garlic clove, and place in the salad bowl.

Into the clabber, whisk the vinegar, salt, sugar, dry mustard, black pepper, and fresh dill. Pour the clabber dressing over the cucumber and onions in the wooden bowl. Toss to mix well, cover with plastic wrap, and chill for 1 hour. Keep refrigerated and use within 2 or 3 days.

Serve on its own as a little salad, or as a bitey accent to accompany other dishes.

MAKES ABOUT 8 CUPS

Fresh Nectarine-Pear-Pineapple Chutney

True Indian chutneys are incendiary-sweet fruit relishes, usually curried, often accented with raisins. Esme's Western-style chutney is pungent-sweet but not fiery. And it is made with easier-to-find ingredients. But like Indian chutneys, it too is made shortly before serving to take full advantage of the fresh fruit flavors. "Cut your fruit coarsely or finely, to give it a chunky-relish or fruit-jam consistency, as you prefer," Esme says. "I'm more the chunky type, I am. Tee-hee."

5 or 6 nectarines (about
    1 1/2 pounds)
2 just-ripe sweet pears
    (about 1 pound)
1 cup diced fresh pineapple
1/2 cup granulated white
    sugar
1/4 cup finely chopped
    sweet onion
1 large clove garlic, minced
1/2 teaspoon grated fresh
    ginger
2 tablespoons white-wine
    vinegar
1 teaspoon curry powder
1/2 teaspoon ground
    cinnamon
1/2 teaspoon salt
Generous pinch ground cloves
Generous pinch cayenne pepper

Wash, pit, and cut the nectarines into bite-size pieces. Peel, core, and cut the pears into bite-size pieces.

In a large nonmetallic saucepan, combine the nectarines, pears, pineapple, and sugar. Cook over medium heat for a few minutes, stirring occasionally, letting the nectarines and pineapple release their juices.

Add the onion, garlic, ginger, vinegar, curry, cinnamon, salt, cloves, and cayenne. Bring just to a boil. Then lower the heat and cook at a simmer, uncovered, 10 to 20 minutes, until the fruit is tender and the liquid has cooked down a fair bit. Stir occasionally, but gently.

Turn into a glass bowl to cool. Taste for seasoning, adding more sugar if necessary. Let steep and season for an hour or so before serving. It will keep for a week in the refrigerator.

This chutney will add a burst of lively flavor to a casserole or mild soup. Spread on a sandwich, mix into salad dressing.

MAKES ABOUT 5 CUPS

Wild Blueberry Jam

"Nine out of ten first prizes in the jams and jellies is more than just luck!" said an admirer as the large and lively Mrs. Hoggett emerged from the county fair with a basket of trophies and blue show ribbons. "Oh well, luck still plays its part," Esme bubbled modestly. "Our berries were wickedly good this year, oh yes. And our water's very tasty, too. We don't use the town water, you know. Rain water from the tanks. It's a much sweeter drop." One more secret: Esme uses the smaller, spicier *wild* blueberries.

10 half-pint canning jars
3 pint baskets wild blueberries or cultivated blueberries
1/4 to 1/2 cup fresh lemon juice
4 cups granulated white sugar
1/4 teaspoon ground allspice
1/4 teaspoon ground cinnamon

In a large pot, place the jars in enough boiling water to cover by 1 inch. Boil 10 minutes. Turn off the heat. Prepare the jar tops according to the manufacturer's directions.

Wash berries well. Place in a large heavy nonmetallic pot, and crush with a potato masher. Stir in just enough lemon juice for a pleasantly tart taste.

Stir in the sugar, allspice, and cinnamon. Bring to a boil, lower heat, and simmer 5 minutes, stirring frequently. Increase heat to high and cook, stirring constantly, until jelly stage, 220° on a jelly thermometer. To make sure jelly has cooked enough to gel: With a spoon, drop a few drops on a chilled plate. Jam should just about set up as it hits the plate—if it does, it's ready; if not, cook a bit longer.

One by one, remove jars from the pot. Pour in boiling jam, leaving 1/4 inch of headspace. Wipe rims clean, put on tops, and screw on bands.

Place sealed jars upright in boiling-water bath, making sure jars are covered by at least 1 inch of water. Bring to full boil, and then boil 5 minutes. Remove jars to a wire rack to cool. Test seals. Label jars, and store in cool pantry.

Now you have a luscious blueberry addition to omelets and sandwiches, or a topping for scones, breads, and muffins. Try it on homemade ice cream—an unequaled treat.

MAKES 10 HALF-PINTS

Mulled Holiday Cider

"It's the time of year when the house is just *perfumed!*" Mrs. Hoggett says. "Arthur puts hickory logs on the fire. My cookies or a pie is baking in the oven. And the sweet spicy smell of mulled cider—that comfy, clovey aroma. I can smell it still in my dear Ma's kitchen, I can." When the grandchildren and all the little cousins come in from playing so hard in the snow all day, chilled to the bone and too dazed to speak, Esme sits them by the fire and wraps their numbed fingers around steaming mugs of mulled cider, and then puts out three more mugs. "For Arthur, me, and the pig!" she says. "The little chap *loves* that clovey smell too. Oh I know he does—pigs smile!"

2 quarts sweet cider
1/2 cup firmly packed brown
   sugar
1/4 teaspoon salt
1 teaspoon ground cloves
1 teaspoon ground allspice
Pinch of grated nutmeg
3 sticks cinnamon

In a large nonmetallic saucepan, combine the cider, sugar, and all the spices, including the cinnamon sticks, and simmer for 10 minutes.

Strain through cheesecloth while still hot. Reheat and serve.

MAKES ABOUT 8 CUPS

Esme's Flavored Whipped Butters

The good woman's sweet butters take her already exalted breads, dinner rolls, and scones to another level. "Start with a pound of butter for each flavor," Esme says. "Always! Oh, it may seem a lot, but it makes sense to prepare a good bit and save it—then you have it. Don't these butters sound devilish?" she says. "Dab them on hot-from-the-oven breads and pastries. *Sin*-ful!"

1 pound unsalted butter,
   softened to consistency
   of putty

ORANGE, LEMON, OR LIME
   1/2 cup honey
   Grated zest and juice of
      either 1 orange,
      2 lemons, or 3 limes

MAPLE OR ORANGE
MARMALADE
   1/3 cup real maple syrup
      or orange marmalade

STRAWBERRY
1 1/4 cup confectioners' sugar
   1/3 cup sliced fresh
      strawberries, mashed

CHOCOLATE
   1 cup confectioners' sugar
   6 tablespoons chocolate syrup

Place the butter in an ample mixing bowl. With an electric mixer fitted with the paddle—not the whip or the dough hook—whip the butter at high speed for 1 to 2 minutes, or until smooth. Then beat in the flavoring ingredients until well blended.

Divide the butter into fourths. Spoon one fourth down the center of a 12-inch sheet of wax paper and, using the paper, squish the butter into a 9-inch long log and wrap tightly. (If butter is too soft to roll, place in refrigerator for 5 minutes or until firm.) Repeat with the remaining butter. Refrigerate for 3 to 4 days, or freeze for up to 6 weeks.

To flavor grilled tomatoes, mashed potatoes, pancakes, warm rice pudding, or anything else your heart desires, just slice off a pat or two, and plop.

MAKES 1 POUND

Something Sweet
from Paradise

"Baking is the soul of country life."

There's no place like a farm for desserts. Trot with Babe through the Hoggett orchards, and he'll point out to you the tree-borne jewels he sees regularly transformed into succulent fruit pies, cakes, cobblers, and sorbets by Mrs. H.'s alchemy. "Our desserts follow the seasons," Esme says, "starting with the first apricots of summer. Then berrying time! Trooping with the grandchildren out to the creek banks on cool early mornings. Oh my! *Worlds* of blackberries, huckleberries, raspberries—my little workers staggering in with gallon buckets full, *demanding* my cobblers and tortes as reward, and righty-oh!" In the fall, crisp apples, sweet tender pears, juicy persimmons ripening seductively on Hoggett trees. Lemons, tangerines in the cooling months. And the first luscious strawberries and rhubarb not until spring. It's true: Having the time to bake seems an outdated luxury to most people; not so on Hoggett Farm. "Are you daft then?" Esme says. Great desserts are an article of faith in the Hoggett cosmos. "Arthur says *of course* there's a Hoggett heaven, and it will have *all* my prize desserts and he'll be allowed to eat them to his heart's content, the dear." For now—a sampling of the rewards the Good might expect to find in Paradise.

Blackberry Cheesecake Torte

Wild blackberries grow along the fence rows of the lane bordering the Hoggett farm, just beyond the reach of the sheep. Thank heaven for small favors, the Boss says to himself every summer as he watches the plump berries ripen. When the time is right, he wades into the bramble patch with a large bucket, while Babe and the sheep dogs Rex and Fly sit patiently and watch. He harvests enough of the biggest, juiciest morsels for Mrs. Hoggett to make his cherished breakfast torte and, he hopes, some preserves. He is *religious* about not eating any of the berries while picking them. But then, on the walk back to the house, he nibbles, oh, one or two, and then more and more . . . until he has to run the final distance to the kitchen to ensure there are any left.

BLACKBERRIES

- 2 pints blackberries, rinsed and drained
- 1/2 cup granulated white sugar
- 1/2 teaspoon ground cinnamon

CRUST

- 1 1/2 cups graham cracker crumbs
- 1/3 cup unsalted butter, softened
- 1/4 cup granulated white sugar

Preheat your oven to 300°.

PREPARING THE BLACKBERRIES: Place the blackberries in an ample bowl. In a small bowl, combine the sugar and cinnamon, and sprinkle over the berries, tumbling and coating them. Let sit 10 minutes, until they become juicy.

MAKING THE CRUST: In a bowl, with a fork, mix together the crumbs, butter, and sugar. Press this mixture evenly over the bottom and up the sides of a 9-inch pie pan. Place an identical pie pan on top and press down firmly, then remove. You'll have an even crumb crust underneath.

MAKING THE FILLING: In an ample bowl, with an electric mixer on medium speed, beat together the cream cheese and sugar until well blended. Then beat in the eggs, one at time. Pour the filling into the crust.

(continued)

FILLING

- 1 package *(8 ounces)* cream cheese, softened
- 1/2 cup granulated white sugar
- 2 large eggs

Bake in the 300° oven 40 minutes, until filling is set.

Remove from the oven and arrange berries on top. Bake 10 minutes, until the sugar on the berries is melted and the berries soften a bit. Let the torte cool partially.

Top with chilled whipped cream if you like, and serve warm. The boss has been known to eat leftovers, cold, for breakfast.

MAKES 8 SERVINGS

Two Sorbets

It is the only time Arthur ever worries about Esme. Whenever they go to town, he is vigilant. It occurs when she moves within reach of that Venus Fly Trap, that opium den of a thousand fascinations for people like Esme—the Different Drummer's Kitchen Supply Store. Esme was bustling around at her usual 90 miles an hour when—"Oh, Esme-e-e!" Kathy the Kitchen-Store Witch smiled, beckoning. Hoggett found his wife half an hour later, and it was bad. She was staring glassy-eyed at it, spellbound, helplessly fondling the knobs. It was a shiny new Garland 8-burner restaurant stove with twin oversize baking ovens. Esme was lost. Arthur spoke gently to her, trying to bring her back, while she babbled how *of course* they could afford it! couldn't do without it! had to have it! not tomorrow but today!... Hoggett was ready. "There's something you *have* to see," he whispered to her, "at the appliance store, right away." He eased Esme out the door and took her down the street to a demonstration of a nice little ice cream machine. Mrs. H. got interested. Arthur bought the machine pronto. A rainbow of sorbets, happily, is now a permanent part of Esme's dessert repertoire. She remembers nothing about a Garland stove. Nothing. It's all a blank.

Persimmon Sorbet

This is the first sorbet Esme made, using fruit from a backyard tree. Try the same technique with strawberries or almost any other raw, fresh fruit. Vary the amount of sugar you use to suit the natural sweetness of the fruit. Keep in mind that persimmons are available from October to February, and there are two kinds available: the Hachiya, which is round with an elongated, slightly pointed end; and the smaller Fuyu, which looks like a tomato. Either way, the taste is deliciously elusive.

7 to 8 persimmons (about 3 pounds)
1/2 cup granulated white sugar
1/2 cup water
2 tablespoons fresh lemon juice

Cut the persimmons in half, and scoop out the pulp. Place the pulp in a food processor, and puree. Scrape into a fine-mesh strainer placed over a bowl, and push the puree through with the rounded bottom of a ladle. Discard any solids left in the strainer.

In a small heavy saucepan, mix sugar and water, and heat over medium-high heat, stirring, until the sugar is dissolved. Let cool a bit, then stir this sugar syrup into the persimmon.

Season with a little of the lemon juice, adding just enough to sharpen the persimmon flavor and balance the sweetness of the sugar. Place in refrigerator to chill, an hour or two.

Pour the chilled mixture into your ice cream maker and freeze, following directions for your machine. Serve immediately, or scrape into a freezer container and store in the freezer compartment of your freezer, or in the ice house.

Garnish with thin strips of citrus zest, if you like.

MAKES ABOUT 2 PINTS

*Port-and-Cabernet Sorbet
and Persimmon Sorbet*

Port-and-Cabernet Sorbet

A zesty, highly flavorful dessert or refreshment. Some have been known to let this melt, and then *sip* it for dessert.

Grated zest (*about 2 teaspoons*) and juice of 1 large orange (*about 1/2 cup*)

1/4 cup Port wine

1 1/4 cups full-bodied Cabernet Sauvignon

Freshly ground black pepper, to taste

3/4 cup granulated white sugar

3/4 cup water

Set up the ice cream maker on the counter for this one.

In a bowl, stir together the orange zest and juice, Port, and Cabernet. Add 8 to 10 grinds of black pepper, and stir in.

In a small heavy saucepan, stir together the sugar and water, and heat over medium-high heat, stirring, until the sugar is dissolved. Let cool a bit, then stir this sugar syrup into the wine mixture.

Place the bowl in the refrigerator until thoroughly chilled, an hour or two.

Pour the chilled wine mixture into your ice cream maker and freeze, following the directions for your machine. When done, scoop into dessert glasses and serve immediately, or scrape into a glass or nonmetallic freezer container and store in the freezer compartment of your freezer, or the ice house.

Garnish with thin strips of citrus zest, and serve vanilla wafers or sugar cookies as the perfect accompaniment.

MAKES ABOUT 1 1/2 PINTS

Great Grandma's Chocolate-Marshmallow Cake with Chocolate Frosting

Home food, Esme calls it. Made from scratch and "rich as the railroad," she says. "And just as easy as a mix, it is—if there were a mix for this treasure, which there isn't!" It's an old, old recipe, of German origin, she thinks, that her mother's mother learned and handed down. "She grew up during the greebly Depression, she did, and they never had enough money for the cup of butter. I grew up during the greebly War, and we never had the sugar!—it was rationed. Oh yes, I always look for any excuse to make this luscious cake. Is it your birthday, dear?"

CAKE

1 1/2 cups all-purpose flour
  1/4 cup unsweetened cocoa
       powder
  3/4 teaspoon salt
    2 cups granulated white
       sugar
    1 cup (2 sticks) unsalted
       butter, softened
    4 large eggs
1 1/2 cups shredded sweetened
       coconut
1 1/2 cups chopped pecans
    1 teaspoon vanilla
    1 package (10 ounces) large
       marshmallows*

Preheat your oven to 350°. Butter a 13 × 9 × 2-inch baking pan—butter is good.

MAKING THE CAKE: Onto a piece of waxed paper, sift together the flour, cocoa powder, and salt. In an ample bowl, with an electric mixer on high speed, beat the sugar and butter until smooth and creamy, about 5 minutes or so. On low speed, beat in the eggs, one at a time.

On low speed, beat the flour mixture into the butter mixture until well blended. With a wooden spoon, stir in the coconut, pecans, and vanilla. Spread the batter into the prepared baking pan.

Bake in the 350° oven for 30 to 35 minutes, or until the top of the cake is set and dry-looking.

Remove the pan from the oven, place on a wire rack, and immediately cover the top of the cake with large

FROSTING

- 1 box (16 ounces) confectioners' sugar
- 1/3 cup unsweetened cocoa powder
- Pinch of salt
- 1/2 cup (1 stick) unsalted butter, softened
- 1/4 cup milk, or less
- 1/2 teaspoon vanilla

marshmallows. Place the cake back in the oven just until the marshmallows melt by about half, 6 minutes or so. They should be puffed and soft. Then remove the pan from the oven again—be sure to use your oven mitts when doing all this—and place on a wire rack to cool.

MAKING THE FROSTING: In a bowl, mix together the confectioners' sugar, cocoa powder, and salt. In a large bowl, with an electric mixer on medium speed, beat the butter until creamy. Gradually beat in the sugar mixture until well blended and smooth. Gradually beat in the milk until the frosting reaches a good spreading consistency. Beat in the vanilla. Spread the frosting over the marshmallow layer.

Cut in squares and place on dessert plates, with homemade vanilla ice cream—or store-bought, which will do in a pinch.

*NOTE: If you are not a big fan of marshmallows, omit them—the cake is absolutely delicious without them. Or, use the mini marshmallows if you like.

MAKES 16 SERVINGS—THIS IS A COMPANY-A-COMIN' DESSERT

Esme's Apple Cake with Dark Rum Sauce

"Been a *real* dry summer . . ." John Larkin, the itinerant knife-sharpener and spinner of "prodigies" was back for another visit. "No lie, over in Cattaraugus County the fire hydrants are pulling themselves loose and chasing dogs." The angular Larkin was sitting with Arthur Hoggett under the silver maple, where they were supposed to be shucking corn and peeling apples and potatoes. "Yep. Fella told me food's so scarce they're making soup from the shadows of crows that starved to death."

Hoggett snorted. Two can play the game. "Back in '38, food was short. We were using mustard plasters to make sandwiches."

"Oh ar. Cattaraugus—worse. Their oat crop is so poorly they're harvesting with nail clippers."

"That'd be a *good* year. We soaped our fields and shaved 'em with razors."

Esme came out of the house, dismayed to see the mouths flapping and the peelers idle. "If you two old fuels don't finish that work, you're going to be getting a plate of dust and a gumball for dinner." She noted the unpeeled apples. "And no apple cake with buttered rum sauce and flavored whipped cream." She marched inside. Larkin got straight to work with his peeler. "Sure I've tasted her apple cake with rum sauce, and it was so rich and agreeable as to be Godlike. Not a word of a lie!"

CAKE

1 cup all-purpose flour
1 teaspoon baking soda
1 teaspoon ground cinnamon
1 teaspoon grated nutmeg
1/2 teaspoon salt
1/4 cup (1/2 stick) unsalted butter, softened

Preheat your oven to 350°. Butter a 9 × 9 × 2-inch square baking pan.

MAKING THE CAKE: In a small bowl, stir together the flour, baking soda, cinnamon, nutmeg, and salt. In an ample bowl, with an electric mixer on medium speed, beat the butter until creamy. Beat in the brown and white sugars until well blended and fluffy, about 3 to 4 minutes. Beat in the eggs,

1/2 cup firmly packed
   brown sugar
1/2 cup granulated
   white sugar
 2 large eggs
 2 teaspoons water
 2 Golden Delicious apples,
   peeled, cored, seeded,
   and coarsely grated
   (about 2 1/2 cups)
1/2 cup chopped walnuts

RUM SAUCE
1/4 cup (1/2 stick) unsalted
   butter
1 1/2 cups firmly packed
   brown sugar
1/2 cup heavy cream
1/4 cup dark rum

WHIPPED CREAM
 1 cup heavy cream
 1 teaspoon vanilla
 2 teaspoons honey or
   maple syrup

one at a time, and the water. On low speed, beat in the flour mixture until well blended.

Fold in the grated apples and chopped walnuts. Spread the batter evenly in the prepared pan.

Bake in the 350° oven for 30 to 35 minutes, or until the cake begins to pull away from the sides of the pan. Transfer the pan to a wire rack to cool.

MAKING THE RUM SAUCE: In a small saucepan, melt the butter, and whisk in the brown sugar and cream. Cook over low heat, whisking now and then, until the sugar is dissolved, about 6 minutes. Set aside to cool. Then stir the dark rum into the cooled butter-sugar sauce.

MAKING THE WHIPPED CREAM: In a small bowl, with an electric mixer on medium speed, beat the heavy cream until soft peaks form. Add the vanilla and the honey or maple syrup for a touch of sweetness.

Cut the apple cake in squares or triangles and place on dessert plates. Spoon a little of the rum sauce over each piece of cake, and top with whipped cream.

MAKES 6 TO 8 SERVINGS

Three Hoggett Cookies—Grandchildren's Choices

Are you baking for show? Is your future mother-in-law coming? Your three most accomplished friends from college? Take the dough by the horns and put a few of Mrs. Hoggett's tricks to work. "*Never* bake on a hot day," Esme says, "everything falls apart. Pie crusts—oh heavens! Only on a clear cool day with low humidity, that's a *rule*. And then the deep dark secret of show baking: Winnowing. With cookies, start by making a double-double batch. Lay out just the best two dozen of these, choosing ones that are the same size, uniform in color. Then pick the very best ten or twelve. Arrange the proud little debutantes on your dessert plate, and . . . "Well I swan! You are a *genius* in the kitchen! My, *my* . . . " The culls? For your real friends.

Pecan Sugar Cookies

These are sugar cookies raised to the power of ten. "Just as simple, they are, too," Esme says, "and ever so much tastier. They'll just *slay* you straight out of the oven."

3/4 cup plus 2 tablespoons
    granulated white sugar
1/2 cup (1 stick) unsalted
    butter, softened
  1 large egg
1/4 teaspoon vanilla extract
  1 cup pastry flour or cake
    flour (note: the pastry flour
    makes for a crisper cookie)
Pinch of salt
  3 tablespoons finely chopped
    pecans
  3 tablespoons brown sugar

In an ample bowl, with an electric mixer on medium speed, beat together the sugar and butter until smooth and creamy, about 2 minutes. On low speed, beat in the egg and vanilla. Beat in the flour and salt until blended into a dough.

Scrape the dough onto a sheet of plastic wrap or waxed paper. Flour your hands (make sure they're clean and dry), and use them to shape the dough into a log, about 10 inches long and 1 1/2 inches in diameter. Wrap the dough up, and refrigerate at least 3 hours or overnight.

When ready to bake, preheat your oven to 350°. Grease a baking sheet. In a pie plate, mix pecans and brown sugar.

Unwrap the dough, and slice 1/4-inch-thick rounds. Press one side of each cookie into the nut mixture, and place, nut side up, on baking sheet, spacing about 1 1/2 inches apart.

Bake in 350° oven until light golden brown around edges, about 8 minutes. Slide the cookies off the sheet onto a rack. Repeat with remaining dough. Store in an airtight container at room temperature.

MAKES ABOUT 3 DOZEN COOKIES

Santa's Jelly Fingers

This is an old-fashioned Mom's recipe that children never leave home without.

COOKIES

    1 cup (2 sticks) unsalted
       butter, softened
3/4 cup firmly packed
       light-brown sugar
    1 large egg yolk (save the
       white—you'll need it
       later in the recipe)
    2 cups sifted all-purpose flour
1/4 teaspoon salt
    1 cup rolled oats or
       quick-cooking oats

DECORATION

    1 large egg white
1 1/2 cups finely chopped
       nutmeats, such as walnuts
       or pecans
About 1/3 cup currant or
       raspberry jelly

Preheat your oven to 350°.

In an ample bowl, with electric mixer on medium speed, beat butter until creamy, 1 minute. Add brown sugar gradually, beating well, 3 to 4 minutes. Beat in yolk. On low speed, beat in flour and salt until blended. Stir in oats.

In a small shallow bowl, lightly beat the egg white. Spread the nuts on a sheet of waxed paper. With your hands, shape pieces of dough into ovals, 1 1/2 × 3/4 inches. Dip each into the beaten white, then roll in chopped nuts.

Place on ungreased baking sheets, spacing them about 2 inches apart. Press an indentation in the center of each with your finger—this will eventually hold the jelly.

Bake in 350° oven 10 minutes. Remove baking sheets from oven, to again press finger indentations into cookies—don't linger here, for the sake of your fingers, and so cookies don't cool too much. Return to oven for 5 more minutes—cookies should be firm and lightly colored on bottoms.

Slide the cookies off the baking sheets onto a wire rack. Let them cool slightly, then fill the indentations with jelly.

And Happy Holidays from Hoggett Farm! Ho, Ho, Ho!

MAKES 3 1/2 DOZEN

Russian Tea Cookies

Pretty, and melt-in-your-mouth delicious—a favorite treat of the czars.

1 cup (2 sticks) unsalted
   butter, softened
1 1/2 cups confectioners' sugar
2 teaspoons vanilla extract
2 cups all-purpose flour
1/4 teaspoon salt
1 cup chopped walnuts

Preheat your oven to 325°.

In an ample bowl, with electric mixer on medium speed, beat butter and 1/2 cup of the confectioners' sugar until well blended and fluffy, about 1 minute. On low speed, beat in the vanilla, flour, salt, and walnuts to make a stiff dough.

With floured hands, break off the dough into 1-tablespoon amounts, and roll lightly between palms into 1-inch balls. Place on large ungreased baking sheet, 1 1/2 inches apart.

Bake in the 325° oven until the cookies are lightly golden on the bottom, about 15 to 20 minutes.

Meanwhile, sift 1/2 cup of the confectioners' sugar onto a platter or a sheet of waxed paper. When the cookies are done, transfer them with a spatula to the confectioners' sugar. While still warm, roll the cookies gently around in the sugar. Sift the remaining confectioners' sugar over the cookies to coat them thoroughly. Let them cool. Store in an airtight container at room temperature.

Serve with freshly brewed coffee and homemade ice cream or sorbet, or just pop one with your breakfast.

MAKES 3 1/2 DOZEN

Easy Holiday Candies

Candy making for the scheduled-up, is what Esme offers here—for busybees who still want to put something deliciously homemade on the dessert sideboard. "These are my 'between-two-doors' candies," she says, "mix them and make them between running in and out." No boiling, no candy thermometer, no soft-ball stage. Just the deep, rich flavors of the home kitchen.

Luscious Maple Creams

"Creamy, buttery, nutty—shouldn't these be outlawed?!" Mrs. H. says. "I have to give myself a good talking to not to eat as I go."

CANDIES

1/2 cup (1 stick) unsalted
    butter, softened
3 tablespoons heavy cream
4 cups confectioners' sugar
3/4 teaspoon maple flavoring
1/2 cup finely chopped walnuts

MAKING THE CANDIES: In an ample bowl, with an electric mixer on medium speed, beat together the butter, cream, 2 cups of the sugar, and the maple flavoring until blended and smooth, about a minute or two. Beat in the remaining sugar and the nuts. Place the whole bowl in the refrigerator to firm up the mixture, for about 45 minutes.

Line a baking sheet with waxed paper. When the candy mixture is firm enough to handle, break off pieces in 1-tablespoon amounts, roll into 1-inch balls, and place on the waxed paper. Try to keep your hands as cool as possible, and handle candies as quickly and as little as possible—and no sampling! All that butter softens quickly. When all the

CHOCOLATE COATING

9 *ounces semisweet chocolate chips*

1 1/2 *squares (1-ounce squares) unsweetened chocolate, coarsely chopped*

3 *teaspoons vegetable oil*

maple creams are on the paper, slide the sheet into the freezer for about a 1/2 hour to get them very cold.

MAKING THE CHOCOLATE COATING: While the maple creams are chilling, place the chocolate chips, unsweetened chocolate, and the oil in the top of a double boiler, and place the top over simmering water. Heat and stir until well mixed and smooth.

Okay, here's the tricky part. Line another baking sheet with waxed paper. Gently spear a chilled maple cream with a fork. Dip into the melted chocolate until thoroughly covered, lift out, and gently tap the fork against the side of the pan to get rid of excess chocolate clinging to the maple cream. Place on the waxed paper-covered sheet. Remove the fork, and seal the holes with a drop of chocolate. Keep on moving. Keep the uncoated creams in the freezer as you work. If the chocolate thickens, reheat gently to thin. When all done, store the coated creams in the refrigerator.

If serving up as a treat or giving as a gift, wrap them in pretty candy papers.

MAKES ABOUT 2 1/2 DOZEN

Brilliant "Candy" Slices

A candy or a cookie? As you please. "I call it a sweetmeat," Esme says. "So pretty, and so-o-o yummy-rich. Eat just one and stop there. Go ahead! Try!"

1 cup (2 sticks) unsalted
    butter, softened
1 cup confectioners' sugar
1 large egg
1 teaspoon vanilla extract
2 1/2 cups all-purpose flour
1 cup chopped walnuts
1 cup green candied cherries,
    cut in halves
1 cup red candied cherries,
    cut in halves

In an ample bowl, with an electric mixer on medium speed, beat together the butter and sugar until smooth and creamy, about 2 minutes. Beat in the egg and vanilla. Then, on low speed, beat in the flour until well blended. Finally, stir in the walnuts, and the green and red candied cherries.

Divide the dough in half. On a piece of plastic wrap or waxed paper, place one half of the dough and shape it into a 10-inch-long log. Wrap up. Repeat with the other half of the dough. Refrigerate both logs for about 2 hours, or until firm enough to slice.

When ready to bake, preheat your oven to 350°. Grease a baking sheet.

Cut the logs into 3/8-inch-thick slices and place on the greased baking sheet, 1 1/2 inches apart.

Bake in the 350° oven until golden brown on the edges, about 10 to 12 minutes. Slide the slices from the baking sheet onto a wire rack to cool. Store in an airtight container at room temperature.

MAKES ABOUT 4 DOZEN

Rummy Yummies

Or Bourbon Balls, if you choose. They're an All-Grownup holiday treat at Hoggett Farm. Babe notices a curious change as the Boss and the Mrs. make them—an escalation in gaiety. He watches the Boss's technique of measuring out the shots of rum or bourbon—one for the candy, one each for the cooks. Could it have anything to do with that? "Well, it's a tradition, it is!" Esme bubbles. Her Cousin Irene reports the Rummy Yummy tradition lives on despite her family's recent move from farm to town, except now her kids call them Suburban Balls. No boiling or baking necessary.

3 cups finely crushed vanilla wafers (about 75 wafers—put them in a heavy-duty plastic bag, and go at it with a rolling pin or the bottom of a heavy skillet)

1/4 cup unsweetened cocoa powder

1 cup confectioners' sugar

1 cup finely chopped pecans

1/4 cup corn syrup

6 to 8 tablespoons rum, bourbon, or brandy

Granulated white or confectioners' sugar (if you prefer) for coating, about 1/4 cup

In a large bowl, stir together the crushed wafers, cocoa powder, sugar, and chopped pecans. Stir in the corn syrup and rum (or bourbon or brandy), adding enough of the liquor so the mixture can be shaped into balls.

Spread the sugar out on a piece of waxed paper. Shape the candy mixture into 1-inch balls, and roll in the sugar. The candies are now ready to eat—no baking. Better to store these at room temperature in an airtight container a day or two or three—the flavor will mellow a bit.

If you fancy a mocha flavor, add a tablespoon or two of instant coffee powder to the mixture.

Don't plan on operating any heavy farm machinery after sampling a few of these.

MAKES ABOUT 4 DOZEN—ENOUGH FOR ALL THE NEIGHBORS, AND THEN SOME

Swedish Rice Pudding with Lingonberries

"Why of course she has the map of Sweden on her face," Mrs. Hoggett says of her dear friend and closest neighbor Marie (a mile and a quarter down the road). The daughter of Swedish parents who took pride in their heritage, Marie gave Esme this recipe reflecting those Scandinavian roots. It is a scrumptious rice pudding spiced with sweet, pungent cardamom and served with lingonberries—cowberries—a slightly tart red fruit native to Sweden. (Cranberry sauce is a good substitute.) Marie's mother served this pudding at light Sunday evening suppers with freshly baked breads, cakes, and cookies, and good Swedish egg coffee. "I learned Hide-the-Almond from Marie," Esme says. "The lucky child—well, now the lucky grandchild—who finds the almond in the pudding gets a lovely prize!"

3	cups water
1 1/4	cups short-grain rice,* uncooked
7	cups milk
6	large eggs
1/2	cup raisins
1/2	cup granulated white sugar
2	tablespoons unsalted butter, melted
1/2	teaspoon vanilla extract
1	teaspoon ground cinnamon
1	teaspoon salt
1/4	teaspoon grated nutmeg

In an ample saucepan, bring the 3 cups of water to a boil. Stir in the rice slowly. Cover and cook over low heat for 20 to 25 minutes, or until tender, uncovering the pot for the last 5 minutes.

In another saucepan, heat 5 cups of the milk to very hot, but not boiling. Stir in the cooked rice and cook for 10 more minutes.

Preheat your oven to 325°.

In a medium-size bowl, lightly beat the eggs. Stir in the 2 remaining cups of cold milk, the raisins, sugar, butter, vanilla, cinnamon, salt, nutmeg, and cardamom.

Remove the rice mixture from the heat. Stir in the egg mixture, then pour into an ungreased 13 × 9 × 2-inch baking dish. Place the dish in a roasting pan and place on an oven

1/4 teaspoon ground
    cardamom
2 cups lingonberries or
    whole-berry cranberry
    sauce

rack. Pour enough boiling water into the roasting pan to come up about 1 inch on the baking dish. Carefully slide the rack into the oven and close the oven door—don't slosh the hot water.

Bake in the 325° oven for 1 1/4 hours, stirring carefully once or twice during the cooking. When you can insert a knife into the center of the pudding and it comes out clean—that's when the pudding is done. Transfer the baking dish to a wire rack to cool.

Spoon squares of pudding onto plates and surround with fresh lingonberries or cranberry sauce. If you like, you can first gently warm the lingonberries in a small saucepan. And, you can serve the pudding warm or cold.

Sprinkle a bit of cinnamon on each serving, or drizzle with heavy cream.

*NOTE: Use short-grain rice. The short grains cook moister and stick together well for molded dishes. (Short-grain rice is popular in Asian cultures for the same reason: Easier to eat with chopsticks.)

MAKES 8 TO 10 SERVINGS

Crêpes with Sautéed Apricots and Toasted Almonds

If you have lived your whole life in Hoggett Hollow, a little green valley somewhere just to the left of the twentieth century, you might never have developed a taste for crêpes. Esme Hoggett, however, fortunate enough to have for fans and correspondents two people who are world-ranking experts in the French crêpe, has developed a world-ranking appetite for the delicious things. Mme. and M. Guy Vaulot, from their village restaurant in the Haute Savoie in southeast France, sent Esme this recipe. "A wonderful dinner-party treat," she says. "Comes together quickly and oh-so-elegantly." Use the same recipe to make apple pie *à la mode* crêpes, with cinnamon, caramel sauce, and vanilla ice cream. Or, another swoon-inducing variation—sautéed strawberries in Grand Marnier topped with whipped cream. "Cold weather, a fire in the fireplace, you giving lovely individual crêpes to your guests. They'll give you the Nobel Prize in Desserts."

CRÊPES

1/4 cup (1/2 stick) unsalted
    butter
2 large eggs
2/3 cup all-purpose flour
Pinch of salt
3/4 cup milk

TOPPING

1/4 cup sliced blanched
    almonds
1/2 cup heavy cream

MAKING THE CRÊPES: In an 8-inch nonstick omelet pan, melt 2 tablespoons of the butter.

In an ample bowl, stir together the eggs, flour, and salt until the batter is smooth. Add the melted butter, and stir it in. While stirring, thin the batter with enough milk to make it smooth and runny. Reserve.

Melt the remaining 2 tablespoons of butter in the omelet pan. Then pour off the butter into a small holding dish.

Place the pan over medium heat until the residual butter begins to sizzle. Pour a scant 3 tablespoons of the batter into the pan, tilting and turning the pan to spread the batter thinly over the entire bottom. Cook the crêpe just until light

1 1/4 *pounds fresh ripe apricots*
       (about 16)

  1/4 *cup (1/2 stick) unsalted*
       butter

  1/3 *cup granulated white*
       sugar

    3 *tablespoons Amaretto*

golden brown on the bottom—45 seconds or so. Flip the crêpe, and cook until golden brown on the other side. Slide the crêpe out of the pan onto your work board and let cool. Lightly re-butter the pan and repeat the operations for subsequent crêpes, thinning the batter with milk if the crêpes are coming out too thick. Stack the crêpes as you go; you should end up with 8.

MAKING THE TOPPING: In a dry skillet, toast the sliced almonds over medium heat until golden brown, about 4 to 5 minutes. Reserve.

In a medium-size bowl, with an electric mixer on medium speed, beat the cream until soft peaks form.

MAKING THE FILLING: Halve and pit the apricots. Cut into 1/2-inch pieces. In an ample skillet, melt the butter. Add the apricot pieces, and sauté over medium heat until the pieces have softened, about 2 to 3 minutes. Add the sugar, and cook, stirring a little, until it is dissolved and the mixture thickens. Remove the pan from the heat and carefully pour in the Amaretto. Return the pan to the heat, and cook for about 30 seconds.

Divide the apricot filling among the 8 crêpes. Fold them over, and place 2 crêpes on each of 4 dessert plates. Top each crêpe with a spoonful of whipped cream and a sprinkle of toasted almonds. Serve immediately.

MAKES 4 SERVINGS (8 CRÊPES)

Uncle Beeson's Butterscotch Pie with Meringue

Uncle Beeson was a great kidder. And a gifted baker. Two talents he put together on one occasion when Esme was a young girl. "Butterscotch Pie!" Esme and her cousins hollered when he opened the floor to requests. It was the closest thing they could imagine to a candy bar. "What's a butterscotch?" one of the younger cousins asked. Uncle Beeson lit up like a bulb. With a grin and a wink—and hot potatoes for each child's pockets to keep the fingers warm—he bundled them all off to the snowy orchards to "see if there are any butterscotches left." By the time the little ones came trooping back in, tired, discouraged—*starved!*—without a single butterscotch to show, Beeson was ready. Surprise! A magnificent meringue-crowned butterscotch pie appeared hot from the oven—turning gloom to laughter. Beeson's gag works only once a generation, but his pie works every time. The perfect winter dessert, it requires no fresh fruit. When it's cold and dark by 3 in the afternoon and spirits need lifting, this warming confection takes folks back to the nursery. "How are the butterscotches this year?!" Esme and the cousins called out to Uncle Beeson each winter as they arrived. "Beautiful! Golden!" he yelled back. "It'll be the best pie ever!" That's no fooling.

FLAKY PIE CRUST
1 1/2 cups all-purpose flour
1/2 teaspoon salt
10 tablespoons solid vegetable shortening, cut into small pieces and chilled, or 5 tablespoons shortening and 5 tablespoons unsalted butter
3 to 4 tablespoons ice water

Place an oven rack in the bottom third of your oven. Preheat your oven to 400°.

MAKING THE PIE CRUST: In an ample bowl, mix flour and salt. With a pastry blender or 2 knives held like a scissors, cut in the shortening until mixture is crumbly. Add ice water, a tablespoon at a time, tossing with a fork, until mixture comes together. Shape the dough into a disk.

On a lightly floured surface, roll out dough into a 13-inch round, about 1/8-inch thick. Fit into a 9-inch pie pan. Trim

CUSTARD

    2 large egg yolks
    1 tablespoon all-purpose
       flour
    Pinch of salt
    1 cup firmly packed
       dark-brown sugar
    1 cup sour cream
    1 teaspoon vanilla extract

MERINGUE

    3 large egg whites
    1/4 teaspoon cream of tartar
    1/2 teaspoon vanilla extract
    6 tablespoons granulated
       white sugar

the overhanging pastry, and make a standup edge. Crimp or flute, as you like.

Bake the crust in the 400° oven for about 10 minutes, or until set and lightly golden. Remove the pan to a wire rack and lower the oven temperature to 325°.

MAKING THE CUSTARD: In a medium-size bowl, with an electric mixer on medium speed, lightly beat the egg yolks. Beat in the flour, salt, and brown sugar until well mixed. Beat in the sour cream and vanilla. Pour into the crust.

Bake in the lower third of the 325° oven for 30 to 40 minutes, or until the custard is firm.

MAKING THE MERINGUE: In a medium-size bowl, with an electric mixer on medium speed and with clean beaters, beat together the egg whites and the cream of tartar until soft peaks form. Beat in the vanilla and the sugar, a tablespoon at a time, until stiff peaks form, but making sure they stay glossy. Do not overbeat and dry out the meringue.

When the custard is set, remove the pie from the oven. Increase oven temperature to 375°, and place the rack in top third of oven. Spoon dollops of meringue on top of the pie, then spread evenly to edges, making sure meringue touches the crust all the way around, sealing the top.

Return the pie to top third of 375° oven, and bake until lightly browned, 12 minutes. Remove to a wire rack to cool.

MAKES 8 TO 10 SERVINGS

Sweet & Tangy Strawberry-Rhubarb Pie

It is a given among the animals that Humans aren't trainable. Maybe stubborn, maybe stupid—it was a big debate between the sheep and cows. But Babe had occasion to put that assumption to the test at the dinner the Mrs. threw for the visiting First High Plenipotentiary of the National Council of Country Women's Associations and her husband. They were just finishing with Esme's heavenly strawberry-rhubarb pie, which the F.H.P. was swooning over. Esme, feeling wickedly flush, served up another perfect slice of the pie on one of her fine china dessert plates, added an elegant twist of whipped cream, and slipped it to Babe in his spot by the kitchen door. Babe sniffed at it delicately, stuck a tentative pink tongue in the juice, and lay down with a sigh. Esme watched mystified—if ever there was a dessert hound it was Babe. She did some deep thinking, oblivious to the *marvelously* humorous story the F.H.P. was telling. Abruptly Esme stood up, whisked the plate to the sink and scraped the pretty wedge of pie onto an ordinary plate. She messed it up a little, tossed in a potato peel, and marched it back to the pig. "Now we're cooking!" exulted Babe, pouncing on the delicious thing with eager snorts and slurps. "Pigs love a leftover!" The Mrs. returned to the table in time to chuckle politely at the punch line of the F.H.P.'s story. Babe lay there smiling with love and appreciation, gratified to know that *his* Human was smart enough to realize that Presentation is All.

FLAKY PIE CRUST

- 1 1/2 cups all-purpose flour
- 1/2 teaspoon salt
- 10 tablespoons solid vegetable shortening
- 3 to 4 tablespoons ice water

Preheat your oven to 450°.

MAKING THE PIE CRUST: In an ample bowl, stir together the flour and salt. Using a pastry blender or 2 knives held like a scissors, cut in the shortening until the mixture is crumbly. Add the ice water, a tablespoon at a time, tossing with a fork, until the dough comes together in a mass. Shape the dough into a ball.

(continued)

FILLING

- 1 *pint small strawberries*
- 2 *cups 1/4-inch diced rhubarb (8 ounces fresh, or 10-ounce package, frozen and thawed)*
- 3/4 *cup granulated white sugar*
- 2 *tablespoons water*
- 3 *tablespoons cornstarch*
- 3 *large egg yolks*
- 1/4 *cup light cream*

WHIPPED CREAM TOPPING

- 1/2 *pint heavy cream*
- 2 *tablespoons granulated white sugar*
- 1/2 *teaspoon vanilla extract*

On a lightly floured surface, roll out the dough into a 13-inch round, 1/8-inch thick. Fit into a 9-inch pie pan. Trim edges and make a standup edge. Crimp or flute edge, as you like. Prick the bottom and sides of crust with a fork.

Bake in the 450° oven until the crust is light golden brown, about 10 minutes. Set aside on a wire rack to cool. You can turn the oven off now.

MAKING THE FILLING: Rinse, hull, and quarter the strawberries, and reserve.

In a heavy medium-size saucepan, combine the rhubarb, sugar, and the water. Bring to boiling over medium-high heat, covered, and stirring occasionally. Reduce the heat and simmer, covered, again stirring occasionally, until the rhubarb is softened, about 4 to 5 minutes.

Meanwhile, in a small bowl, stir together the cornstarch, yolks, and light cream until very well blended. When the rhubarb is softened, stir a little of the hot rhubarb mixture into the yolk mixture. Now, stir the yolk mixture into the rhubarb mixture in the saucepan. Over medium-low heat, stir the filling until bubbly and thickened, a minute or two. Then simmer for 1 minute more. Remove from the heat, and stir in the strawberries. Let the filling cool slightly, about 10 minutes. Then pour the filling into the crust, and place in the refrigerator to chill and set, 3 to 4 hours.

MAKING THE TOPPING: When ready to serve, in a chilled bowl, combine the heavy cream, sugar, and vanilla. With an electric mixer on medium speed, beat the cream until soft peaks form. Spoon a dollop on each serving.

For a final flourish, place a perfect strawberry on each plate.

MAKES 6 TO 8 SERVINGS

Ferdie's Chocolate Bread Pudding

"QUACK! Get away from there!... Get out! Get out!... Shoo, you!" That was Ferdinand, the insecure duck, trying to make himself indispensable tearing around the barnyard, chasing hens away from the flower garden, mice from the barn, the pet rabbit out of the kitchen patch. "Don't wanna be dinner!... Be unpalatable!" He did a 360 in the mud and came up filthy. And running—after a stray dog ambling up the lane. "QUA-AA-ACK! Beat it, you mange!" Mrs. Hoggett looked up from a favorite read, *Aunt Babette's Cook Book*, and watched the neurotic spectacle. "My goodness, what is with that fowl?!" she thought. As she returned to her ancient tome, a verse hit her eye: "We may live without love—what is passion but pining? But where is the creature can live without dining?" She eyed the frantic duck. "Food *is* love," she mused. "Ma always said so." She went inside, took a steaming dish from the oven, and spooned out a goodly portion of her deeply rich, chocolatey bread pudding. She lavished it with whipped cream and summoned the duck to dine. Ferdinand was Flabbergasted! Thrilled! Tickled Pink! to be so gloriously singled out. "Kisskisskisskiss!" he kept saying to Esme in Duck. He gorged himself on the creamy, toothy ambrosia and fell blissfully asleep on the fence rail, dreaming of long life. Esme sighed her thanks for the silence, and for the wondrous power of warm chocolate pudding to smooth the wimpled wing of care.

(*continued*)

PUDDING

1/4 cup (1/2 stick) unsalted
     butter
2 large eggs
2 cups milk
1 teaspoon vanilla extract
1/2 cup unsweetened cocoa
     powder
1 cup granulated white
     sugar
2 cups 1-inch pieces fresh
     bread and crusts

WHIPPED CREAM

1 pint heavy whipping
     cream
1 teaspoon granulated
     white sugar
3 to 4 drops vanilla extract

Preheat your oven to 300°. Use a tablespoon of the butter to grease a 6-cup baking dish—an 8 1/2 × 3 5/8 × 2 5/8-inch baking dish or even a soufflé dish.

MAKING THE PUDDING: Cut the remaining butter into small pieces, and reserve. In an ample bowl, stir together the eggs, milk, and vanilla. In a small bowl, stir together the cocoa powder and sugar, and then stir into the egg mixture until well blended.

With a spatula, gently fold the bread into the pudding mix. Do not over overmix. Pour into the buttered baking dish. Top with dots of the remaining butter.

Bake in the 300° oven for 50 to 60 minutes, or until set.

Remove the pudding from the oven, and while still hot, stir the pudding with a fork for a minute or so to even out the consistency and break up the lumps of bread. Let sit on a wire rack to cool.

MAKING THE WHIPPED CREAM: In an ample bowl, with an electric mixer on medium speed, beat together the cream, sugar, and vanilla until soft peaks form.

Serve the pudding warm, or chilled. Spoon into dessert goblets or pudding dishes, and top with a dollop of whipped cream, or even just chilled heavy cream.

MAKES 6 TO 8 SERVINGS

Fresh Carrot-Coconut Cake with Whipped Molasses Frosting

There is no mistaking this came out of a farm kitchen rather than a cardboard box. "Why, it's lusher than any commercial carrot cake that's ever passed your lips," Esme says. "Start with a good carrot, oh yes. Any size carrot, as long as it's sweet! Taste is the test. And firm, with splendid orangy color. And no cracks! Cracks mean a woody core." Served warm straight from the oven, this cake is intoxicating. Tightly wrapped and saved, it will grow magically even more moist and luscious with a day or so of seasoning. One Esme secret: "Baking soda. I use soda because baking *powder* contains a moisture absorber which makes for a drier and lighter-colored crumb. The *soda* gives a lovely dark color and a much moister crumb. Oh well, never mind all the greebly science. What matters is, it works!"

CAKE

- 2 *cups all-purpose flour*
- 2 *teaspoons baking soda*
- 2 *teaspoons ground cinnamon*
- 1 *teaspoon salt*
- 4 *large eggs*
- 2 *cups granulated white sugar*
- 1 1/2 *cups vegetable oil*
- 3 *cups shredded carrots*
- 1/2 *cup flaked sweetened coconut*
- 1/2 *cup chopped walnuts*

Grease a 9-inch springform pan or 9 × 9 × 2-inch square baking pan. Preheat your oven to 375° for springform pan, or 350° for square pan.

MAKING THE CAKE: In an ample bowl, stir together the flour, baking soda, cinnamon, and salt.

In another bowl, with an electric mixer on medium speed, beat together the eggs and sugar until well blended. Add the flour mixture to the egg-and-sugar mixture, and beat well on low speed. It will be thick. Add the vegetable oil in a thread, beating well again until everything is mixed together. Stir in the carrots, coconut, and walnuts, and mix well. Spread the batter into the prepared baking pan.

(continued)

WHIPPED MOLASSES
FROSTING

1 1/2 *tablespoon molasses*
  1 *container (12 ounces)*
    whipped cream cheese
  2 *to 3 tablespoons*
    confectioners' sugar

Bake springform in 375° oven for 70 minutes, or square pan in 350° oven for 50 to 60 minutes, or until the cake pulls slightly away from the pan sides.

Let cake cool in the pan on a wire rack. Release and remove the side of the springform pan, or turn cake out of the square pan. The top of the round cake will dip slightly.

MAKING THE FROSTING: In a small bowl, mix the molasses into the whipped cream cheese. Then stir in the confectioners' sugar, to taste. Spread the frosting over the top and sides of the cake.

A glass of cold milk and a piece of this moist cake— that's almost a meal.

MAKES 8 TO 10 SERVINGS

Blue Ribbon Raspberry-Peach Cobbler

One day Babe gathered all the animals under the kitchen window to listen to Mrs. Hoggett talking to herself as she bustled to finish baking for the country fair. Perhaps they could learn something. "A 'cobbler'—now, that's a baked fruit dessert with a crust, but it's not a pie, oh no, because it has a top crust only and no bottom," she said. "Usually. Whereas a pie *always* has a bottom crust, a side crust, and sometimes a top. A 'crisp' though, has a crusty top that is not a cobbler crust, which is dough, but a layer of crumbly buttered crumbs. A 'buckle,' mind you, has a crumbly crust on top that isn't a crisp at all, but a streusel. You see? Then again I prefer a 'betty,' which is lovely spiced fruit *between* layers of crispy buttered bread crumbles and not ever to be confused with a 'pandowdy,' which was first made in the 1600s and is similar to a cobbler except that . . ." The animals stumbled back to their accustomed barnyard places, dazed. Moral: Some knowledge hurts the head too much to get.

1 pint raspberries, fresh, or frozen, thawed (blueberries are good, too)

1 large perfectly ripe peach, peeled, pitted, and thinly sliced

2 tablespoons granulated white sugar

Juice from 1/2 lemon (about 1 tablespoon)

1/4 cup (1/2 stick) unsalted butter, softened

1/2 cup granulated white sugar

1/2 cup milk

1 cup all-purpose flour

1/4 teaspoon baking powder

1/4 teaspoon salt

Preheat your oven to 375°. Butter a 9 × 5 × 3-inch loaf pan.

In an ample bowl, toss together the berries, peach slices, the 2 tablespoons sugar, and the lemon juice.

In another bowl, ample as well, with an electric mixer on medium speed, beat together the butter and the 1/2 cup sugar until blended. Beat in the milk.

In a separate bowl, mix flour, baking powder, and salt. On low speed, beat the flour mixture into the butter mixture until a thick batter forms. Turn about three-quarters of the batter into the prepared pan. Spoon the berry mixture over the batter. With a spoon, drop remaining batter in globs over fruit—hence the cobbled look, and thus the dessert's name.

Bake in the 375° oven for 45 to 50 minutes, or until the fruit is bubbly and the cobbled top is golden brown. Spoon onto dessert plates while still warm.

Great with just a dribbling of chilled heavy cream—or a scoop of homemade vanilla ice cream.

MAKES 6 SERVINGS

Acknowledgments

My very special thanks to Nancy Cushing-Jones at Universal Publishing Rights for inventing this book and inviting me to write it. Her staunch belief in the project, her cool-headed support at every turn, and her deft editorial guidance were bolstering to me, much appreciated, and central to the outcome. All credit, if Babe's little book amounts to a hill of beans, goes to Nancy.

Cindy Chang was a constant source of support and good cheer throughout as Universal's flight-deck commander and nimble trouble-shooter. A thousand thanks, Cindy.

A lion's share of gratitude goes to the many home cooks, listed below, who generously contributed favorite family recipes to this book. Without them, nothing. This is their book, their cooking and, in fictionalized form, their country lore and stories.

I am especially and forever indebted to a warm-hearted farm cook and retired educator from Maplewood, Minnesota, Honor Hacker. As well as sharing with me her recipes and knowledge, she gave me access to a netwrok of other farm cooks and their family recipes. Thanks to Honor, her husband Joe and daughter Mary Dolores for a treasure trove of lore, anecdotes, and good will.

My undying thanks to my friend and cooking mentor, Ken Frank, who recently re-incarnated his acclaimed Los Angeles restaurant, La Toque, in Rutherford in the Napa Valley. Ken not only gave me a number of superb original recipes for the book, but was there at the other end of the phone at all hours to answer questions, solve problems, provide ideas, and offer moral support. He was unstintingly helpful. I am in his debt.

I am abidingly grateful to my wife Nancy for her patience and wise counsel, and to my children, Maggie, Nell, and Lucy for providing me inspiration as well as headnote ideas, and for putting up with my materials spread all over the family room for months.

Leslie Stoker and Tom Klusaritz saw the potential in a Babe cookbook. I salute Leslie's excellent editorial instincts, as well as her Babe-attuned sense of humor. Barbara Marks designed the book, giving clear and pleasing form to the raw materials. David Ricketts took expert charge of testing the recipes and was a strong presence at the end stages of the book, knitting up culinary loose ends.

Special thanks to Ayala Elnekave for her sage vegetarian insights and guidance.

Thank you:

Jacqueline Orr Miller, Elsie K. Muske and her daughter Carol Muske-Dukes, Joan Brzezinski and her daughter Lynda King, Aunt Marion King, Kris Kuss, Lori Haynes, Mary Dee Hacker, Rita Hacker, Dorothy Stotts and her daughter Diane Haager, Kathy Ernst, Jane Gram, Susan Fusiara, Gloria Hunt and her daughter Nancy, Cora Boyle, Margaret Gram, Karen Pope Chieffo, Bea Grabowski, Rosemary Meyer, Jean Rohlik, Vicki Klima, Phyllis Hamill, Julie Schwalback, Yvonne McCumber, Polly Malley, Mary Dougherty Pavlovich, Shelia Boyd, Brother Francis Carr, Marie Oberg, Irene Huot, Joan Rada, Virginia Kennedy Conway, Lorraine Sabatini, Kate Jackson, Thank you all.

Lastly, thanks to my agent Peter Turner for his seminal role in getting this project airborn, for his timely encouragements, and for his sure-handed, behind-the-curtain ministrations making the crooked straight, the rough smooth.

—DEWEY GRAM

Metric Conversions

WEIGHT EQUIVALENTS

The metric weights given in this chart are not exact equivalents, but have been rounded up or down slightly to make measuring easier.

AVOIRDUPOIS	METRIC
1/4 oz	7 g
1/2 oz	15 g
1 oz	30 g
2 oz	60 g
3 oz	90 g
4 oz	115 g
5 oz	150 g
6 oz	175 g
7 oz	200 g
8 oz (1/2 lb)	225 g
9 oz	250 g
10 oz	300 g
11 oz	325 g
12 oz	350 g
13 oz	375 g
14 oz	400 g
15 oz	425 g
16 oz (1 lb)	450 g
1 lb 2 oz	500 g
1 1/2 lb	750 g
2 lb	900 g
2 1/4 lb	1 kg
3 lb	1.4 kg
4 lb	1.8 kg
4 1/2 lb	2 kg

VOLUME EQUIVALENTS

These are not exact equivalents for the American cups and spoons, but have been rounded up or down slightly to make measuring easier.

AMERICAN	METRIC	IMPERIAL
1/4 t	1.25 ml	
1/2 t	2.5 ml	
1 t	5 ml	
1/2 T (1 1/2 t)	7.5 ml	
1 T (3 t)	15 ml	
1/4 cup (4 T)	60 ml	2 fl oz
1/3 cup (5 T)	75 ml	2 1/2 fl oz
1/2 cup (8 T)	125 ml	4 fl oz
2/3 cup (10 T)	150 ml	5 fl oz (1/4 pint)
3/4 cup (12 T)	175 ml	6 fl oz (1/3 pint)
1 cup (16 T)	250 ml	8 fl oz
1 1/4 cups	300 ml	10 fl oz (1/2 pint)
1 1/2 cups	350 ml	12 fl oz
1 pint (2 cups)	500 ml	16 fl oz
2 1/2 cups	625 ml	20 fl oz (1 pint)
1 quart (4 cups)	1 litre	1 3/4 pints

OVEN TEMPERATURE EQUIVALENTS

OVEN	°F.	°C.	GAS MARK
very cool	250–275	130–140	1/2–1
cool	300	150	2
warm	325	170	3
moderate	350	180	4
moderately hot	375	190	5
	400	200	6
hot	425	220	7
very hot	450	230	8
	475	250	9

Index